OWN IT

OWN IT

NAVIGATING THE COLLEGE ATHLETE EXPERIENCE TO A SUCCESSFUL CAREER & LIFE

JESSICA COOK

NEW DEGREE PRESS

COPYRIGHT © 2019 JESSICA COOK

All rights reserved.

OWN IT

Navigating the College Athlete Experience to a Successful Career & Life

ISBN   978-1-64137-335-7   *Paperback*

        978-1-64137-650-1   *Ebook*

To my Mom, who has been teaching me to
***OWN IT** ever since I was a little girl.*

*To my Dad, who always encouraged me to **OWN IT***
on the softball field & in other areas of my life.

*To Carolyn, who inspires me to **OWN IT** no*
matter how challenging the task.

*To Matthew, who motivates me to **OWN IT***
in each of my daily endeavors.

CONTENTS

INTRODUCTION

———

Five years of college after a redshirt, transferred schools, all these years of high school, all these years before high school just for this moment.

—RYAN GILLIAM, FORMER STUDENT-ATHLETE
AT THE UNIVERSITY OF SOUTH FLORIDA

Ryan Gilliam dreamed of going to the NFL. Those who grow up and play football in Tallahassee, Florida, share this dream, and most of the time that dream turns into a reality. Of course, Tallahassee is a main stage for high school football, perhaps the most real-life version of *Friday Night Lights*. Although Ryan was a multi-sport athlete growing up, football was his true passion.

He attended Lincoln High School, the second-best high school football program in the nation. He, along with his friends, planned to make it into the NFL together.

The odds were in their favor.

* * *

More than **490,000** students yearly compete at the collegiate level in a variety of **24** sports. This number accounts for all levels of NCAA competition; a little over **1,100** institutions fall under the NCAA's umbrella.[1]

College athletics itself is a billion-dollar business. Not a million. A *billion.* Wrap your head around that. The March Madness tournament alone generates approximately **$900 million** in revenue.[2]

Many share a common misconception that most college athletes are trying to take their skills to the next level and become professionals in their sport.

This notion, however, is not true or possible.

---

1   NCAA.org - The Official Site of the NCAA. (n.d.). *Student-Athletes.*
2   Parker, T. (2019). *What Does the NCAA Really Net from March Madness?.* Investopedia.

About **8 out of every 10** student-athletes will earn a bachelor's degree, and **35%** of those students will go on to attain a postgraduate degree.[3]

According to the NCAA, only **2%** of all college athletes will go on to play professional sports, leaving **98%** of student-athletes to find jobs elsewhere.[4]

Two percent.

* * *

Ryan was going to be in that **2%**. He knew it.

After multiple successful high school football seasons, Ryan and a good portion of his teammates went on to play football at Division I schools. Taking his talents across the country, he attended the University of Oregon.

Ryan's goal was to make a name for himself in the football world.

At Oregon, he earned a spot on the field as a starter. After seeing the talent and success of his teammates, Ryan quickly determined

---

3   NCAA.org - The Official Site of the NCAA. (n.d.). *Student-Athletes*.
4   Ncaa.org. (2018).

that he could not make the plays he needed to be successful. Thus, he came to the conclusion that he should head back to his home state. Ryan decided to attend the University of South Florida and spent the remainder of his college football career at USF; he would even be given the chance to potentially play in the NFL.

"I knew all I had to do was make big plays in big games and I was going to finally get my shot to be in the league with my friends," Ryan said.

During his junior year, Ryan's NFL football career came down to one single play. USF was playing Auburn and a bunch of NFL scouts were at the game to watch Mike Jenkins, a teammate of Ryan's who was the top-rated player coming out of college. He ended up playing in the NFL for eight years, mostly with the Dallas Cowboys. Mike made all the plays he needed to make during that game to pave his path to the NFL. Now it was Ryan's turn.

The game was in the fourth quarter of the nationally televised game; USF and Auburn were tied 17-17. Auburn was faced with third down and twelve yards to go for a first down. Auburn was already in field goal range, so this next play was going to be huge.

"I already knew based on the call that we were going to blitz, and I was going to have my opportunity to make a play. Little did I know it was going to be a play that was going to define my entire career," Ryan described.

With all eyes on USF, Ryan knew exactly what play Auburn was going to run.

The ball was snapped, the pass was thrown, and it was coming right to Ryan. As the ball spun through the air, Ryan prepared himself to make the interception. All of a sudden, he dropped the ball.

Ryan did everything right but catch the football. He said, *"Five years of college after a redshirt, transferred schools, all these years of high school, all these years before high school just for this moment, just to prove that I actually deserve to be in the league, I deserve to have a shot to be right along with my friends because we were going to the league together—and I dropped the ball. Like, seriously?"*

Ryan thought his professional career was over, but he was about to find out he was wrong.[5]

* * *

Pro Football Hall of Famer Jerry Rice preaches in the NCAA student-athlete commercial that you have to plan for life after sports.[6] But listening to that advice is difficult when so many

---

5   Gilliam, R. (2018). *Tallahassee Dreams*. [video].
6   NCAA TV Commercial, 'Opportunity' Featuring Jerry Rice. (2016). [image].

external forces tell you otherwise—recruiters, coaches, team-mates, friends, family.

The student should come before the athlete, not the other way around. Some people have the perception that Division I student-athletes do not ever have to attend class, which is also hardly true.

If **98%** of student-athletes are not becoming professional athletes, we should emphasize the importance of athletes being in class to help prepare them for life after graduation.

And we are often told college coaches do not care how their student-athletes perform in the classroom as long as they remain eligible.

There may be some truth to this, but for the most part, coaches want what is best for their athletes. Knowing that most of their players will not become professional athletes, coaches realize that student-athletes need to perform well in the classroom so that they can graduate and become successful in something other than sports.

* * *

Ryan became a successful professional, just not in football.

He now fell into the category of the **98%**.

After the USF vs. Auburn game, Ryan lost his confidence and did not know exactly what he was going to do with his life after college. Then Lee Roy Selmon walked into his life. *The* Lee Roy Selmon, as Ryan says. Selmon was a Pro Football Hall of Famer who told Ryan something that rocked him to his core. Ryan recalled, "He said the same work ethic, the same energy, the same passion that I put into football I can put into other areas and different careers. He said if I was half as good as I ever thought I was, if I had any type of integrity or character, any type of discipline and focus I could be just as good at business as I was at football, even better." Ryan started to believe that Selmon was right and this moment marked the turning point for him.[7]

After taking Selmon's advice, Ryan concluded that he wanted to be a businessman. However, he faced one slight problem. Ryan was a criminology major who knew hardly anything about business. Selmon explained to Ryan that all he had to do was learn the basics and outwork the people around him to be successful—which is exactly what Ryan did. He found an entry-level job, crushed it, and moved his way up the business ladder, accepting a promotion within six weeks of being hired.

---

7   Gilliam, R. (2018). *Tallahassee Dreams*. [video].

At age twenty-five, Ryan and his wife started their company, which became very successful. "I realized Lee Roy Selmon was right, all you have to do is grind," Ryan explained.

It doesn't matter what you grind in as long as you put the work in, as long as you have the drive and determination, you do not have to be limited to any one area. ... It doesn't matter what people see you as—as long as you are willing to do the work in another area, as long you are focused and determined, you are going to accomplish whatever you want to accomplish.

Ryan ultimately attributes his drive and motivation to be successful to his time as a student-athlete. The NCAA now uses him as a resource for student-athletes, because **98%** of student-athletes can relate to his scenario.

* * *

According to several studies, student-athletes have a higher chance of obtaining professional success later in life compared to non-student-athletes. *Fortune* estimates that **95%** of Fortune 500 CEOs were college athletes.[8] In addition, college athletics can teach many life lessons that translate into the professional workforce, which is something I can echo from my personal student-athlete experience.

---

8   Johnson, H. (2018). *A look at the link between playing sports and success in business.* The CEO Magazine.

The truth is that most NCAA student-athletes are like Ryan Gilliam, rather than college basketball phenom Zion Williamson.

That's why you must **OWN** your student-athlete experience. Don't let it own you.

As a senior in college, I felt compelled to start this book because I wish I had known all these aspects of student-athlete life before I entered college. I wish someone would have been real with me about the highs and lows of college athletics. Drawing on my student-athlete experience and the experiences of other collegiate athletes and professionals in the industry, I created this book to serve as a guide.

If you **OWN IT** from the moment you step on campus, you will make the most out of your student-athlete experience. Each letter of **OWN IT** represents skills and characteristics you can utilize to successfully navigate the journey of being a collegiate athlete:

- Openness
- Willpower
- Nerve
- Introspection
- Teamwork

You only get four years. Four years to play the sport you love while simultaneously getting a degree in a major you are passionate about.

Within these four years, the lessons learned, skills gained, and friendships made will help you excel in various areas of life. You will be better prepared to tackle the challenges life throws at you compared to non-athletes because odds are you experienced something similar while playing your sport.

In this book you'll gain insight and advice from:

- Kendall Spencer, a former standout student-athlete and national champion in the long jump.

- Beth Brooke-Marciniak, a pioneer for female collegiate athletes and former global vice chairwoman of public policy at Ernst & Young.

- Dominique Moceanu, a member of the 1996 "Magnificent Seven" who won gold in Atlanta.

- Antonio Neves, a former committed Division I athlete and author of *Student Athlete 101*.

With this book, you will become more than prepared to **OWN IT**, not only during your time as a student-athlete but also in your future endeavors. If you are a future collegiate athlete, you will gain an understanding of what to expect as you embark on the journey of college athletics and how you can make the most of it. If you are a current collegiate athlete, this book will teach you how to enhance your current experience. If you are a former student-athlete, you will understand how you can leverage your college athlete experience to discover success in your career and life.

If you aren't careful and don't take your collegiate student-athlete experience seriously, you won't be prepared to leverage yourself after graduation. The point is, **OWN** your student-athlete experience—don't let it **OWN** you.

Of **490,000** student-athletes, **9,800** of them may get their chance to take their athletic talents to the professional level. **480,200** will not. **480,200** student-athletes need to be prepared to successfully navigate their professional careers and lives once they are done playing their sport. **OWN**ing their collegiate athlete experience will help them to do just that.

So, what are you waiting for?

It's time to figure out how to make the most of your student-athlete experience and how you can use it to help drive success in your life.

HOW TO OWN
THIS BOOK

Depending on who you are, you can **OWN** this book in a different way.

The million-dollar question is: how do you want to **OWN** this book?

PROSPECTIVE STUDENT-ATHLETES

What an exciting time for you! Having the opportunity to take your academic and athletic abilities to the next level is truly something special. Odds are that playing your sport in college is something you have been dreaming of and working toward for a long time. Now that dream is becoming a reality.

Although you have likely been an athlete for a good portion of your life, college takes it to a whole new level.

- Your time commitment to your sport increases.
- Your academic coursework increases.
- And, for the first time, you are living on your own.

That's a lot of change.

Use this book as an opportunity to learn from those who have been there and done that. By doing so, you'll be prepared to take on the collegiate student-athlete experience from the moment you step on campus.

Don't get me wrong—you are still going to face your fair share of challenges and obstacles, but you will be prepared to face them head-on and **OWN IT**.

CURRENT STUDENT-ATHLETES

Congratulations, you made it! You are part of a very small percentage of high school athletes who go on to play in college. That's something special.

You understand the daily grind that goes into being a collegiate student-athlete and you understand how challenging it can be. Now that you know what it is like, you probably recognize your strengths and weaknesses as a student-athlete.

The most challenging part of being a student-athlete is the time demands.

There are simply not enough hours in a day to tackle:

- Schoolwork,
- Extracurriculars,
- Practices and games.

Use this book as a tool to help you improve and find balance. Capitalize on your strengths and build upon your weaknesses. Even if you feel as though you are doing the college athlete experience completely right, you still have room for improvement and more ways to **OWN IT.**

FORMER STUDENT-ATHLETES

Four years go by fast, don't they? You will experience no stranger and more emotional feeling than playing your sport competitively for the final time. Regardless of whether you're ready to hang it up, once you are done playing you feel as though a piece of you is missing. This experience is normal.

You know what they say: "One door closes and another one opens." Your next door has opened and it's time for you to OWN IT.

As a former college athlete, you are more than equipped to handle your next endeavor. The great thing about sports is that you learn so much from playing them:

- Life lessons,
- Mental toughness,
- Physical and transferable skills.

You name it, sports have taught you it.

Now you just need to use what you have learned from sports so you can continue to **OWN IT** in your career and life. Use this book as a guide to help you find a way to incorporate the lessons learned and skills gained from your student-athlete experience.

COACHES AND ADMINISTRATORS

You play a significant role in the transformation of many student-athletes' lives. The lessons and skills you teach them are ones they carry with them for the rest of their lives.

That's how much of an impact you make.

You have four years to teach them:

- About their sport,
- About themselves,
- And about their future.

You have a lot to do, but that's what you are trained for.

Use this book to help your student-athletes make the most out of their four years because as we all know, it goes quickly.

You have the tools to help your athletes **OWN IT.**

PARENTS OF STUDENT-ATHLETES

Parents, you have been there for the whole journey, from the moment your athlete started playing sports to their recruiting process and departure for college. You have been their endless support system. If not for you, your student-athlete might not be where they are today.

And now your student-athlete needs your continued support through college:

- Through the transition from high school to college,
- Through the ups and downs of playing the sport they love,
- Through the transition from college to the real world.

It's a pivotal time for your student-athlete, so you need to understand what they are going through. By reading this book, you will get a better idea. Help them **OWN IT** through this transformative time.

PART I

THE
MISCONCEPTIONS

CHAPTER 1

DUMB JOCK

———

I've failed over and over again in my life, and that is why I succeed.

—MICHAEL JORDAN, SIX-TIME NBA CHAMPION[9]

The stereotypical *jock*: an athlete whose mind constantly revolves around sports and is intellectually lacking.

We see this stereotype in movies and read about it in books. I can picture it now: an athlete sitting in a classroom, sporting a letterman jacket and hardly paying attention to what the teacher has to say. Such an image features in movies because

———

9   Competitive Advantage: Mental Toughness. (n.d.). *Competitive Advantage Sports Quote.*

it is viewed as relatable and factual, because society views athletes that way.

The stereotypical idea of a jock dates back to ancient Roman times and Greek civilizations because the Romans held athletic and artistic aspirations at the same level as academics.[10]

During this time period, you were either an athlete, an artist, or an intellectual, but you couldn't be more than one.

Unfortunately, society cannot seem to escape this pervasive stereotype.

You hear it time and time again: "dumb jock." The perception that athletes are intellectually inferior persists today.

A study published by Johns Hopkins University Press analyzes the negative stigma surrounding athletes along with their susceptibility to these negative stereotypes. Male student-athletes, particularly in revenue-producing sports, face these stereotypes more often than other athletes.[11] This statistic makes sense because college football and basketball players experience more media coverage. The media helps

---

10 Barrett, J. (2017). *The Equinox – The stereotype of athletes: Dumb Jock Syndrome*. The Equinox.
11 Feltz, D., Schneider, R., Hwang, S. and Skogsberg, N. (2013). Predictors of Collegiate

reinforce these stereotypes, but so do fans, professors, and other students on campus. The most common misconceptions about college athletes include the idea that student-athletes have other people do their schoolwork, that rules do not apply to them, and that they plan on incorporating sports into all they do in life.[12]

* * *

During my time as a student-athlete, I found myself challenged by some of the generalized misunderstandings about athletes from both students and professors, and I played softball at a small university in Cleveland, Ohio. I cannot even imagine the stereotypes associated with athletes at big Division I schools, especially in sports that regularly attract heavy media coverage.

A lot of my professors and classmates did not understand the pressure heaped on you by being a student and an athlete simultaneously. Knowing that I essentially had a target on my back, however, forced me to work harder to put the stereotypes to rest.

Some professors would give me a hard time about continually missing class because of games rescheduled due to inclement

---

12 Buhler, D. (n.d.). *The Most Common Stereotypes About Student Athletes, Debunked*. Study Breaks.

weather. I couldn't help it, but I was still held responsible for it. After proving myself to my professors and fellow students on campus, I showed them I was not just the typical jock they may have originally expected. I know a lot of other student-athletes go through the same thing.

People tend to be hypercritical of you if you are an athlete, seemingly without rhyme or reason; that's just how it is.

In fact, these stereotypes put student-athletes at a disadvantage from the moment they step onto their college campus. Society's perception of athletes has been permanently distorted. The reality indicates that the misconceptions associated with athletes are not accurate.

At some institutions, sports teams have a higher graduation rate than the school as a whole. For example, the men's basketball teams at both Xavier University and the University of Dayton had graduation percentages higher than their institution's rate. Xavier basketball posted a rate of **78%**, whereas the university as a whole generated a percentage of **75%**. Dayton basketball yielded a **91%** graduation percentage, and the school came in at **77%**, disproving the "dumb jock" stereotype.[13]

---

13   Sheingold, D. (2017). *NCAA basketball: Graduation rates for all 64 tournament teams.* Northjersey.com.

Now, I am not suggesting that such statistics apply to every student-athlete. How could we forget former Ohio State quarterback Cardale Jones' famous tweet stating, "We ain't come to play SCHOOL"?[14]

Why should we have to go to class if we came here to play FOOTBALL, we ain't come to play SCHOOL, classes are POINTLESS (5 October 2012)

—CARDALE JONES @CORDALE10

Unfortunately for student-athletes, this tweet provided non-athletes and professors ammo to use against us. It contributed to the idea that all collegiate athletes attended university solely for their sport. Although this scenario may ring true for a very small percentage of student-athletes, it does not do the majority of student-athletes justice.

To show you the numbers, Division I has about **179,000** student-athletes, Division II has **122,000**, and Division III has **191,000**.[15] Division III, where no athletic scholarships are offered, has the highest number of participants of the three divisions, emphasizing the idea the majority of student-athletes do come to "play SCHOOL."

---

14 Anon, (2015). [image].
15 Ncaa.org. (2018).

Fortunately for some student-athletes, they know their athletic skill has the potential to take them to the next level professionally. Good for them for recognizing their talents early on and chasing after their dreams!

Unfortunately for the rest of us, we have the talent to carry us only through the collegiate level, not the professional level—as is the case with **98%** of collegiate student-athletes in all divisions.

That said, **98%** of us cannot all be classified as "dumb jocks," and the other **2%** shouldn't have that label either. If **98%** of us were really "dumb jocks," we would not be able to experience professional success in careers post-graduation.

Being a student-athlete sets us up to be successful, as many studies have found.

One study published in the *Journal of Leadership & Organizational Studies* concluded that former high school and collegiate athletes attain higher-status careers compared to non-athletes.[16] Additionally, former athletes have the potential to earn between **5 to 15%** more in their life than non-athletes.[17]

---

16 Kniffin, K., Wansink, B. and Shimizu, M. (2014). Sports at Work. Journal of Leadership & Organizational Studies, 22(2), pp.217-230.

17 USA TODAY High School Sports. (2017). *6 reasons former athletes find success after college.*

Did I mention that research shows athletes tend to perform better in school compared to non-athletes?

Well, it's true.

A study published by the University of Kentucky examined the academic performance of athletes compared to non-athletes. Overall, it pointed to the significant differences in academic performance, favoring the athletes. Better grades lead to a higher rate of graduation too. The researchers, Angela Lumpkin and Rebecca Achen, explained, "The potential for sport participation to improve graduation rates, keep students in school longer and increase daily attendance should lead administrators to adamantly support interscholastic sport."[18]

＊ ＊ ＊

Being a collegiate athlete is something special, not something that should be degraded by the phrase "dumb jock," as it has been for years. It's an opportunity that only about 7% of high school athletes are lucky enough to receive.[19]

---

18 Krings, M. (2014). *Study shows high school athletes perform better in school, persist to graduation more than non-athletes.* The University of Kansas.

19 ScholarshipStats.com. (n.d.). *Odds of playing a college sport from high school.*

Only 7%.

You are a part of the small percentage with the opportunity to play the sport you are passionate about at the next level while becoming knowledgeable in an area of study that genuinely interests you.

Such a feat is not something that just anyone can do.

It's time to put the stereotypes to rest.

CHAPTER 2

OWNING THE STUDENT-ATHLETE EXPERIENCE

———

Success is peace of mind attained only through self-satisfaction in knowing you've made the effort to do the best of which you are capable.

—JOHN WOODEN, FORMER UCLA BASKETBALL COACH WHO LED HIS TEAM TO WIN TEN NATIONAL CHAMPIONSHIPS[20]

When I think of college athletic greats, the legendary coach John Wooden certainly comes to mind.

———

20 Stricherz, A. (n.d.). Words John Wooden Never Used. [Blog] *Sports & Spirituality.*

Wooden was a driven and successful basketball coach at UCLA. During his time, he coached his team to ten national titles in a timely matter of twelve years. Wooden is someone I truly believe helped shape college athletics. He worked hard on the development of each and every player to help make them successful once their time at UCLA was over, regardless of whether they were going on to become play professionally.

To do this successfully, Wooden had three rules: never be late, no profanity, and never criticize a teammate.[21] He tried to instill these rules early on in his players to create a positive culture in his program and prepare his athletes for their future.

"I always tried to make the youngsters feel that they're there to get an education, number one," Wooden said in his TED Talk. "Basketball was second because it was paying their way. They do need a little time for social activities, but you let social activities take a little precedence over the other two, and you're not going to have any very long."[22]

Wooden wanted his athletes to remain focused, but he understood the importance of social activities for developmental purposes.

---

21 John Wooden: The difference between winning and succeeding. (2001). [video].
22 Ibid.

To say that John Wooden loved teaching would be an understatement. He deeply valued education. He enjoyed teaching academically and he took his teaching style with him in his role as a basketball coach. To reach and teach as many people as he could, he developed the Pyramid of Success, which consists of fifteen different elements. I found essentially all of them applicable to the student-athlete experience and life afterward as well.

* * *

For success as a student-athlete, you must take command of your experience from the moment you step on campus, especially with the misconceptions and stereotypes putting you at a disadvantage from the start. Being prepared to face your time as a collegiate athlete head-on will help you make the most out of your experience.

The student-athlete experience is truly unique. No other campus organization or club puts its members through what student-athletes do: the time commitment, the traveling, and the pressure, especially when a sport is in its main season. According to the NCAA, in-season sports can practice a maximum of **20 hours** per week, which breaks down to about **4 hours** a day.[23] These numbers do not even account for playing games and associated travel time.

---

23 Ncaa.org. (n.d.). *Countable Athletically Relatable Activities.*

Because of these extensive time demands and other factors, you will be more prepared for what work and life will throw at you simply from being an athlete.

Researchers have studied this phenomenon.

According to *USA Today*, former athletes develop invaluable workplace skills, which cannot be taught easily.[24] These skills are developed after years of practice, which athletes gain through playing sports.

You only have four years of eligibility, so you might as well make the most out of it.

This reality brings me to one simple piece of advice: **OWN IT.**

This mantra applies to both athletics and academics, as well as your years beyond college.

You focus on **OWN**ing **IT** while you are a collegiate athlete, and once you transition into your professional career, you continue to do the same.

---

24 USA TODAY High School Sports. (2017). 6 reasons former athletes find success after college. [online] Available at: https://usatodayhss.com/2017/6-reasons-former-athletes-find-success-after-college [Accessed 22 Sep. 2019].

OWN IT is all about taking the reins on your collegiate student-athlete experience and using it to help you navigate yourself to a successful career and life once athletics is over. **OWN IT** not only serves as a helpful phrase but also provides a structural way for you to make the most of your student-athlete experience.

OWN IT stands for five specific and meaningful words:

- Openness
- Willpower
- Nerve
- Introspection
- Teamwork

Using these five skills individually, as well as simultaneously, yields the recipe for a memorable and successful student-athlete experience that will help you prepare for a successful career and life. Throughout this book, I will reference and analyze elements of John Wooden's Pyramid of Success to fully emphasize how you can discover success as a current or former student-athlete through a variety of different characteristics that correspond with **OWN IT**.

* * *

O IS FOR OPENNESS:

Looking back on my time in college, I wish I had stayed open-minded during my freshman year. My mind was very set and closed-off to change. Once I altered my mindset, I significantly enhanced my student-athlete experience.

Being open-minded and open to new experiences is essentially how the collegiate athlete journey begins. You were open to embarking on the college recruiting process. Then you were open to exploring all your options to decide on the school you felt would suit you best. Once you are on campus and practicing with your team, you have to be open to your coach's style, because no coach approaches the position exactly the same.

So, as athletes, we are somewhat familiar with the idea of being open, but openness becomes even more crucial once you step onto your college campus, especially outside of your sport.

I am not going to sugarcoat it: the transition from high school to college can be rough. You go from being a big fish in a small pond to a tiny fish in a really large pond. Naturally, this transition can cause us to close ourselves off, whether we fully realize it or not.

Everyone does it, even if you do not mean to.

College provides a plethora of opportunities you would not even think you would get. But the catch is that you have to be open to stepping outside your comfort zone. Being open will help to get you to the next level—athletically, academically, and professionally.

W IS FOR WILLPOWER:

Willpower is defined as "control of one's impulses and actions; self-control."[25]

As a college athlete, you must exert control on a daily basis. Being a student-athlete is all about sacrifice. With your demanding schedule, you may find it extremely challenging to fit every single thing you want to do in one day. For me, the majority of the sacrifices I had to make were in my social life.

It takes willpower to make these sacrifices day in and day out, especially for four continuous years.

Willpower is most necessary during times of adversity.

As athletes, we are constantly faced with hurdles to overcome. Whether facing an injury or being benched, we have to figure out how to cope and brainstorm what we can do to change an

---

25   www.dictionary.com. (n.d.). *Definition of willpower | Dictionary.com.*

outcome. Demonstrating your willpower will help to shape your character during your time as a student-athlete. Your character that develops during challenging times will carry with you into your life post-graduation.

N IS FOR NERVE:

Nerve builds upon willpower. It takes nerve to be a student-athlete and it also takes nerve to demonstrate willpower during times of adversity. You need to possess strong willpower to have the nerve to speak up about the various challenges you will face as a student-athlete. You must learn to speak up for what is right for you and your fellow student-athletes.

Use your nerve to help you reach your goals.

Communication is one way to do so and a critical skill for college athletes. But it takes nerve to gain the confidence to communicate your thoughts efficiently and effectively. Think about how many people you come in contact with as a college athlete: coaches, athletic administrators, trainers, professors, and classmates. If you have a message you are trying to convey to all of these people, you must communicate effectively.

You will have to demonstrate nerve even after your time as an athlete draws to a close. Communication is a skill employers look for too. Being a student-athlete will help you to find your nerve, which will translate positively into other areas of your life.

I IS FOR INTROSPECTION:

Introspection is the process of examining, observing, or reflecting on yourself.

You may be thinking: "How the heck is this going to contribute to my student-athlete experience?"

It sounds a little bizarre, but trust me, it plays a role.

As athletes, we are often blinded by the many things happening around us: schoolwork, practices, games, coaching decisions. Feeling that way is understandable, but being slightly more observant of things outside your normal realm of focus can make a big difference.

It's all about knowing yourself and the world around you, paired with an understanding of who you are and what you're passionate about.

Introspection also allows you to see and understand how you can combine your passions and adapt them for you and your goals, perhaps even later on in life as well. Doing so lets you align your passions with your goals, which is not something everyone can accomplish.

Use introspection as a tool to help you understand more about yourself.

T IS FOR TEAMWORK:

"Teamwork makes the dream work."

Society throws this phrase around, but it fully resonates with us as athletes.

Although I am sure you think you know exactly what teamwork is all about, college athletics takes it to a whole other level. Any college team requires many moving parts to operate smoothly and successfully, which goes for not only coaches and athletic administrators, but also players.

Each player, regardless of if you are a starter or on a practice squad, has a designated role and specific purpose. Think of it as your specific job for your team.

For your team to operate like a well-oiled machine, you have to be completing your job to your fullest potential, not worrying about anyone else's role. And, sure, you may find it challenging at times.

How easy is it to get wrapped up in the little things that hardly have any effect on us?

Real easy.

Knowing your role and understanding your purpose will help your team accomplish its goals. In addition, it will help you prepare for the professional work world. The teamwork skills generated from playing sports are applicable to essentially every occupation.

The key is to take these skills you've learned and use them to enhance yourself professionally.

Let's dive in so you can start **OWN**ing your time as a collegiate athlete and be prepared for your life afterward.

PART II

THE OWN IT STRUCTURE

CHAPTER 3

OPENNESS

—

A comfort zone is a beautiful place, but nothing ever grows there.

—UNKNOWN[26]

This quotation is one of my favorites. I apply it to all aspects of my life, especially exercise and professional development.

As humans, we strive to be comfortable in every way we can; we've been conditioned that way:

- Physically
- Mentally
- Professionally
- Financially

---

26 What's Possible... (n.d.). *Favorite Quotes.*

We are always seeking comfort.

Now, don't get me wrong: no better feeling exists than one of comfort with yourself and your surroundings. But, like the quote says, comfort zones do not promote or produce growth.

During my senior year of college, I was asked to speak at the Graduate at Graduation series, a student-organized initiative to help underclassmen make the most out of their college experience by hearing stories and lessons from graduating seniors. This speaker panel began during my senior year.

After participating in it, I realized how beneficial it would have been for me to attend as an underclassman.

In my talk, I emphasized three points:

- The importance of stepping outside of your comfort zone,

- The importance of becoming involved on campus, and

- The importance of fully immersing yourself in the college experience.

Each of these points I discussed relates to being open in a different way. Openness is something that I recognized as a necessity for every college student during my senior year, regardless of whether you're an athlete.

In fact, multiple other students found this topic important enough to mention in their own speeches, proving its relevance and importance in the college setting.

For student-athletes, however, openness is an even greater necessity.

As athletes, we tend to focus solely on our sport, which is easy to do because it has been a constant throughout our lives. We've always had our sport. Not to mention, our sport is what we value and feel passionate about.

Why wouldn't we focus on it?

As a freshman student-athlete, no matter what division you are competing in, you come in focused more on your sport and less on your academics. That's just how it is. After being recruited by a college coach to play, you feel obligated to give it your full, complete, and undivided attention. Eventually, once you get settled into a routine, you'll be able to divvy up your attention slightly more, but your sport will continue to remain a main priority for you.

I did not realize this early on in my college athletic career. I stepped onto John Carroll University's campus ready to play softball, not necessarily ready to focus on my schoolwork. For softball, our primary season is during the spring, but we always had a miniature fall season. Wanting to excel at softball and earn a starting position applied pressure from the start of my collegiate career.

Most student-athletes experience this scenario as well. Athletes who play fall sports come into college during the summer to start training for their sport. By the time classes start, they are already fully focused and locked into their sport, and only their sport. At that point, how could they not give it their undivided attention?

Evidently, such a mindset does not demonstrate the concept of openness.

* * *

Let's go back to the story of Ryan Gilliam, the USF football player who was able to find success outside of his sport.

Ryan was holding the road map to help get him to his dream of playing in the NFL. While chasing this dream, he had to remain open. He was especially open when it came to the college recruiting process. Ryan initially committed to Florida

State University, like many other football players from his hometown but didn't limit his opportunities there.

As a result, he decided he would have a better playing opportunity at the University of Oregon. Then, once Ryan discovered what was best for him and his football career, he transferred to USF. During his transition from Oregon to USF, Ryan had to be open to different coaching and playing styles.

However, the one thing that Ryan did not open himself up to throughout his student-athlete experience was being anything other than an NFL player.

When Ryan realized his NFL dreams were ruined, he was lost.

He was going to graduate in the spring and did not have a plan other than playing professional football.

Throughout his time as a student-athlete, Ryan had tunnel vision on making it to the NFL. He wasn't open to any other options because that was his dream. When he needed guidance, Lee Roy Selmon walked into his life at just the right time. Selmon helped Ryan become open to opportunities outside of football because he saw potential in Ryan that he was unable to see in himself.

When Ryan became open and accepting of Selmon's advice, he was able to make a positive change.

Ryan, a criminology major at USF, made the executive decision that he wanted to be a businessman. To live this out, he pursued an entry-level job in sales.

With an open mind going into his new career and a new perspective on the professional work world, Ryan saw instant success and got a promotion six weeks after starting.[27]

Six weeks. That's all it took.

Even though he started out low on the totem pole, Ryan kept an open mind and continued to work hard. From there, he was able to achieve professional success outside of football, something he would have never imagined doing while he was chasing his NFL dream.

From this success, Ryan went on to do even greater things. He worked his way up the corporate ladder and is now a successful entrepreneur.

The NCAA has also recognized Ryan's success outside of sports. He serves as an advisory board member for After the Game Task Force, a committee created by the NCAA to connect companies with former student-athletes seeking professional opportunities.

---

27   Gilliam, R. (2018). *Tallahassee Dreams*. [video].

Going into college, Ryan put all his eggs in one basket while striving to reach his NFL dream. He did not reach his lifelong goal, but he adjusted his plans and found a way to channel his competitive mentality into another career path that he was passionate about.

He became open to new opportunities.

Ultimately, this mindset propelled him to his success.

* * *

The cool thing about playing sports is that you can learn so much, as long as you are open to it. Think of it as your athletic education.

Erin McDermott, director of athletics and recreation at the University of Chicago, discussed this idea with me.

Erin started playing sports early in her life. She was a multi-sport athlete until she eventually discovered that basketball was her athletic passion. Erin was unsure, however, if she wanted to take her skills to the collegiate level. After some serious consideration, she decided to give it a shot and chose Hofstra University in Long Island, New York.

Erin found that she valued what sports had taught her.

"What I really always valued and took away from my athlete experience was the person that I came to be through the leadership and instincts that I developed," Erin explained.

What Erin is referring to is her athletic education.

Erin became open to the idea of playing college basketball. From there, she became open to the concepts that being a student-athlete would teach her. You should treat the skills and lessons you can learn from playing sports the same way you would treat your school material. Erin attributes her role as a leader to her time as a student-athlete because she feels it taught her how to become an effective leader.

Now, as an athletic director, Erin wants her athletes at the University of Chicago to learn from their athletic education and take it with them into whatever career they desire.

As an athlete, you learn every day. Consider your teammates, coaches, trainers, and administrators to be your teachers.

My college softball coach, Nicole Loudin, and I have also talked about this. Having the perspectives of both a former student-athlete and a coach allowed Coach Loudin to see the importance of what playing and coaching a sport can teach you. For her, being an athlete taught her three specific characteristics:

- Resiliency,
- Respect,
- Creativity.

She would never have acquired these skills and characteristics if she didn't remain open to learning throughout her athletic career. Coach Loudin obtained these skills through her various coaches and teammates on each team she was on. Think about it: each coach you have throughout your time as an athlete has a different coaching style. If you take the time to learn at least one thing from each coach you have, you will be able to develop a unique and diversified skill set for yourself that you can draw on beyond your years as an athlete. Now, as a college softball coach, Nicole Loudin applies the skills she gained as a student-athlete and uses them in her career regularly.

* * *

Being open and stepping outside of your comfort zone can be challenging, and it definitely was for me too.

However, once I took the initial step, I felt a positive impact almost instantly.

When I first got to college, I was confident in my pitching ability—then it came time for my first time to pitch with my pitching coach, Coach Anderson, at practice. Pitching a softball is challenging because it is very technique-heavy. Even more difficult, though, is that every pitching coach has their own style they like to teach. Coach Anderson provided me with a different technique to test out, one very different from mine. I was immediately frazzled and overwhelmed. I was throwing pitches not even close to the strike zone and wanted to go back to my old ways.

But I kept working at it, and as I kept practicing, I started to see a positive effect. The difference was that I had not originally been open to changing my mechanics. After some serious conversations with my parents and teammates, I realized I needed to change my mindset. Once I became open to giving his style a serious try, I saw improvements in my pitch speed and break.

Being open and accepting does not solely apply to your sport. It is a tool that should be used within every area of your student-athlete experience.

For me, openness included taking a class outside of my major, my comfort zone. If I never did that, I would have never become as interested in entrepreneurship as I am, I would have never become as close with certain faculty members at my institution, and I would most certainly not be writing this book. But all because I took one step outside of my comfort zone, I was able to obtain all these additional parts of my student-athlete experience.

Taking these steps toward openness within the student portion of my student-athlete experience helped me to enhance the athletic side as well. I became an overall happier person in both the student and athlete aspects of my life.

Just like Ryan, I became open to opportunities outside of my initial streamlined thoughts and goals.

Like I mentioned, we are accustomed to seeking comfort.

Let's become comfortable with being uncomfortable and stepping outside of our comfort zones.

CHAPTER 4

OPEN FOR THE FUTURE

———

I don't know what my future holds, but I know who holds my future.

—TIM TEBOW, FORMER NFL QUARTERBACK AND
PROFESSIONAL BASEBALL PLAYER[28]

Becoming comfortable with stepping outside of your comfort zone takes practice. It is a weird feeling and not a skill that can be taught and perfected overnight. In fact, it can take periods of trial and error in order to become fully comfortable with it. You might be good at pushing your boundaries within your sport, but when it comes to a social or academic setting, you take a step back. This isn't uncommon.

---

28 Wiepert, G. (2013).

In the life of a student-athlete, comfort zones are regularly tested, because college athletes are constantly faced with change and a lot of the time it happens all at once. Coaching, teammate, and institutional changes are just a few to mention.

And we know that making the step to be a collegiate student-athlete is a major lifestyle change in and of itself.

College students, in general, face many instances of change throughout their four years.

To put into perspective, the U.S. Department of Education reported that approximately **33%** of students enrolled in a four-year education program change their majors[29] From my own college experience, I would have guessed the percentage was higher—that's how common I found major changes to be on my campus.

Try adding switching majors into the mix of other changes student-athletes face.

During this time of significant change comes the opportunity to positively change yourself. College is truly all about the personal transformation process, but this transformation is only truly successful if you remain open and willing to experiencing it.

---

29 Nces.ed.gov. (2017). *Beginning College Students Who Change Their Majors Within 3 Years of Enrollment.*

Lee Reed, director of athletics at Georgetown University, has had his fair share of experiences that ultimately led him to his current role today. Today, Lee would not be as successful professionally if he did not keep an open mind during and after his time as a student-athlete.

Lee began his student-athlete career at Cleveland State University, where he played basketball. He was a starter and eventually worked his way up to team captain. Despite this success, he ended up transferring to the University of New Mexico during his senior year. This decision made sense for him because he was going to be coaching basketball there after graduation.

Lee stayed at the university as an assistant basketball coach for about four years but came to the realization that he was not fulfilled by it. Since he was unsure about his next move, Lee decided to transition into the family business; at the time, it felt like the right thing to do.

This choice was a safe option for him to turn to.

After fully immersing himself in the family business for eight years, Lee realized he was not satisfied by this career either. However, this epiphany did not occur until he was in his early thirties. He knew he needed to find a professional career that would make him happy and one he would be passionate about for the rest of his life.

After a lot of thought and reflection, Lee decided to go back to school to get his master's degree in sport management from the University of New Mexico. This move was pivotal for Lee's professional career path because he was able to discover a genuine enjoyment for the interaction between the administration and student-athletes.

Shortly after receiving his master's in a specialty he felt passion for, Lee made his return to his alma mater, Cleveland State University, where he became the athletic director. This position excited him because of the great experience he had as an athlete at the school. In his new role, Lee vowed to make positive changes to the athletic department, which he certainly did over his tenure. Five teams won championships between 2007 and 2008. That year is considered the most successful year in the school's athletic history. Lee also became a member of several national committees within the college athletics scene.

Eight successful years later, in 2010, Lee made the move to Georgetown University and has been the athletic director ever since. This pivotal career advancement required a move to the Washington, D.C. area for his family, who were

Cleveland-based. Such a step was necessary, however, for Lee to reach his career goals.

Lee Reed did not attain the athletic director position at Georgetown until he was forty-seven years old. Perhaps he would have never gotten this role if he did not go through the process that he did. Before he decided to pursue sports management, choosing a career path was a trial-and-error period for Lee. But he was open to experiencing it.

* * *

"You don't know if you don't try."

That's my motto.

This expression describes what Lee Reed did to discover a profession he felt passionate about. Trying something and determining that you do not like it will help you to learn the things you do like. However, this approach really only works well if you remain open throughout the process, no matter how difficult or challenging it may be.

In his thirties, Lee recognized that he needed to find a career that would fulfill him. However old you are, if you remain open to new opportunities and remain true to yourself, you will find exactly what you are looking for—or perhaps even something you did not know you were looking for.

Testing out your different interests, along with different career paths, will help you uncover your strengths and weaknesses. As I mentioned in the previous chapter, during my junior year of college I became interested in the entrepreneurship department at John Carroll. So, I tested out my interest by taking an introductory-level entrepreneurship course, which validated my interest in the subject. I would have never realized my passion for it if I had never tested out a class. By doing so, I was also able to discover that creativity was a strength of mine while public speaking was a weakness. But, after recognizing public speaking as a weakness, I was able to work with myself to turn it into a strength after some serious practice.

Relating to the athlete side of things, I found my pitch movement to be a strength and my pitch speed to be a weakness once I got to college. So, I worked hard to further enhance my strength and worked even harder to improve upon my weakness.

By being open and accepting of your strengths and weaknesses, you'll be able to improve yourself, both in your sport and also in other various areas of your life.

* * *

The point is: it's okay that you may not know exactly what you want to do with your life when you're in college.

How can anyone expect you to know exactly what you want to do for the rest of your life when you're eighteen years old?

One of the most frequent areas of change that adults experience involves their career. According to an article on The Balance Careers, most people change their profession between three and seven times during their life.[30]

So, if that's the norm, how can you as an eighteen-year-old entering college know exactly what you want to do for your entire life?

You can't.

However, you can be open to the change that will come throughout your professional career. That's what Lee Reed did, and his approach worked out extremely well for him.

At John Carroll University, I needed an internship to graduate from my program of study. During my junior year, I started looking for opportunities that truly interested me. I hardly had a clue what my professional goals were. What

---

30 Rosenberg McKay, D. (2019). *How Often Do People Change Careers?*. The Balance Careers.

helped me to find an internship was using my interests, strengths, and weaknesses that I had previously identified. Once I established these as guidelines, I was able to find an opportunity that was perfect for me.

Although my internship wasn't directly related to my area of study, I gained many valuable skills that I know will help me in any profession I decide to pursue throughout my life. This benefit wouldn't have been possible if I didn't have an open mind while learning throughout my eleven-week internship.

* * *

The concept of openness is similar to John Wooden's idea of alertness in the Pyramid of Success. Wooden describes alertness as such: "Observe constantly. Stay open-minded. Be eager to learn and improve."[31] Keeping your head on a swivel and continuing to observe will help you open your mind and discover new things—things you may have never even known interested you.

In addition, you will learn more from observing than you may think. "There is activity going on around us at all times from which we can acquire knowledge if we have Alertness. Too

---

31 Coach John Wooden. (2019). *Pyramid of Success - Coach John Wooden.*

often we get tunnel vision and don't see the full picture which precludes learning things that are available," Wooden stated.[32]

Being open is transformative. Whether within your sport or in your professional development, openness will help you to grow.

It worked for Ryan Gilliam, Lee Reed, and me. I know it can work for you too.

So, step outside of your comfort zone and discover how to make the most out of the student-athlete experience.

OPENNESS TAKEAWAYS:

- Take steps outside of your comfort zone.
- Test out your different interests to validate them.
- Do not be afraid of change.

---

32 Cawsey, B. (2016). How to apply Coach John Wooden's Pyramid of Success principles to running. [Blog] *Bri Cawsey*.

CHAPTER 5

WILLPOWER

———

Always make a total effort, even when the odds are against you.

—ARNOLD PALMER, ONE OF THE
GREATEST TO EVER PLAY GOLF[33]

One of the greatest takeaways that sports can teach is how to deal with adversity. If you start playing sports at a young age, you learn this quickly. Although it may not seem like a good thing when you are going through a tumultuous time, it is all a learning experience that will ultimately help to shape you as a person.

---

33 BrainyQuote. (n.d.). *Arnold Palmer Quotes.*

In keeping with the **OWN IT** structure, demonstrating will-power comes next. Willpower is all about effectively controlling your actions.

This one is important for all athletes.

Our actions are often a direct reflection of our emotions.

As athletes, we are very passionate people. That's a given.

Athletes are also constantly experiencing change and expected to adapt accordingly, regardless of whether the change is for better or worse. Whether facing coaching changes, life changes, or athletic-related injuries that change how we play, athletes must battle adversity and overcome challenges.

As such, student-athletes must be prepared to handle even more adversity than the average college student.

As collegiate athletes, we are faced with challenges in both the student and athlete aspects of our lives.

* * *

I had the opportunity to speak with gymnast Dominique Moceanu, a gold medalist in the 1996 Olympics.

Dominique became very well-versed in demonstrating will-power from a young age.

Dominique earned her gold medal at the age of fourteen, which is unheard of today. She was a part of the "Magnificent Seven." Because she was in the limelight at such a young age, she was forced to grow up and mature faster than a typical fourteen-year-old would have to.

When discussing character growth, Dominique told me, "The lotus flower blossoms in the dirt and into something colorful after it has gone through all of that dirt."

Referring to adversity, she means that tough times are difficult, but they help us to grow and progress.

However, experiencing and overcoming challenging times takes willpower.

Dominique endured injuries and conflicts from her beloved sport, which required her to face several instances of adversity head-on. In fact, she even competed in the 1996 Olympics with an injury.

After winning gold, her relationship with world-renowned gymnastic coaches Marta and Bela Karolyi was terminated for personal reasons. The Karolyis had trained Dominique for most of her life. After this split, she switched coaches several times throughout her career. Her husband, Dr. Michael Canales, was even her coach at one point during her gymnastics comeback. Dominique ended up competing off and on until 2006, at the age of twenty-four, but she decided that it was time to hang it up after that.

Deciding to retire from a sport that was the main focal point in her life for so long was most definitely a challenging decision to make. Coming to this conclusion alone took willpower.

At seventeen years of age, Dominique first demonstrated willpower in a scenario that is quite difficult to imagine. She had to be strong and use her willpower against her own parents. She sought legal emancipation because she said her parents had "squandered" her earnings from her successful gymnastics career. This personal and legal crisis took a big toll on Dominique and caused her to stop training for a significant period of time.

Imagine finding the willpower within yourself to fight for what is right for you. Now imagine adding your parents into the equation.

This choice was not easy for Dominique to make, but she dug deep and mustered the willpower to fight for her own rights.

This challenge, along with all the others she faced throughout her career, helped shape her character.

"Being an athlete certainly shaped me. ... It was a part of my growth and a part of my life, but gymnastics has been a beautiful blessing. I've always been grateful to have been a part of a sport that forced me to grow so much and challenged me in so many ways," Dominique noted.

Athletes, more often than not, constantly meet challenges, some positive and some negative. However, these obstacles are only preparing you for what's to come in the future.

Now, I am not saying you are constantly going to be faced with adversity when you are done being a student-athlete. What I am saying is that you will be better equipped to tackle challenges when they arise later in your professional career and life.

The lawsuit between Dominique and her parents only helped ready her for a much larger matter later on in her life.

Recently, USA Gymnastics has come under fire for the treatment of its athletes. This controversy not only encompasses the way the coaches treated the gymnasts but also how former team doctor Larry Nassar treated them. Nassar was recently convicted for serial child molestation and sexual assault, using his high-profile position as an avenue to do so. Nassar abused approximately 160 girls and women in the sport, resulting in 40 to 175 years in prison.[34]

The recent accusations against USA Gymnastics were something Dominique had warned people about ten years prior to Nassar's trial. "For the last ten years, I spoke up. I said something when I finally had the courage to in 2008. I recognized how dangerous this culture was; it was headed down a very dark road," she said.

As a result, Dominique testified before the U.S. Senate in an attempt to pass new legislation that would ultimately make sports safer for young athletes while establishing mandatory reporting. The legislation passed and new laws are currently established.

Dominique has continued to show immense willpower in moments when she needed a voice, even once she was removed from the sport.

Despite her demonstrating willpower on a national stage, my favorite way Dominique harnessed her willpower was in her education. After being a successful Olympian, she made the decision to attend college at John Carroll

---

34 Hobson, W. (2018). Larry Nassar, former USA Gymnastics doctor, sentenced to 40-175 years for sex crimes. *The Washington Post.*

University to pursue a degree in business administration. She didn't decide to do so, however, until she was married and had children.

Think about what kind of willpower it would take to balance a marriage, children, and schoolwork.

From there, Dominique went on to become the first college graduate in her family. She always had somewhat of an entrepreneurial spirit, and in 2018 she opened the Dominique Moceanu Gymnastic Center.

None of these accomplishments would have been possible if Dominique didn't utilize her willpower throughout various points of her life.

* * *

Now, I understand that Dominique Moceanu's story is unique and uncommon, but the same principles are still applicable to the life of a collegiate athlete.

As student-athletes, we are constantly faced with adversity and expected to overcome it without question or hesitation.

That's just who we are and what people expect.

This past softball season was one full of challenges, to say the least. My coach's mom received a serious cancer diagnosis at the very beginning of the season, which put an understandable strain on my coach. This news, in turn, affected our whole team. At the same time, we were not performing well. We were hitting pop-ups, dropping fly balls, and giving up a lot of runs every game. I probably had the worst ERA I've ever had in my entire life. It was just an all-around challenging season for everyone, and that can happen. That's what sports are all about. But we were able to finish out the season on a strong note by getting a win. We overcame the adversity and obstacles that we had faced all season to get one final win and finish on somewhat of a high note.

It even happens in Major League Baseball. In the 2019 season, Chris Davis of the Baltimore Orioles went 0 for 49 at-bats.[35] Adversity can also be faced collectively as a team: in the same season, the Pittsburgh Pirates only won 4 out of 28 games after the All-Star Break.

The professionals face adversity just like we, as student-athletes, do.

* * *

---

35 WTOP. (2019). *Davis sets record at 0 for 49, including warning track shot | WTOP.*

Athletes are known for their ability to regularly surmount hurdles. An article published by Athlete Network outlines five aspects of overcoming adversity that athletes can actually teach others:

- Flexibility,
- Persistence,
- Mental Fortitude,
- Perspective,
- Humility.[36]

These are just a few of the qualities that help to make student-athletes highly sought-after employees.

Although Dominique Moceanu was not a student-athlete, the importance of demonstrating willpower is still a lesson we can learn from her journey.

Sports can be a vehicle to shape character through experience and overcoming adversity. Whether it is getting benched by your coach or facing a career-ending injury, everything happens for a reason, even if you don't know or understand the reason at the time. Use any hurdle as an opportunity to learn, grow, and shape your character.

---

36 Smith, C. (n.d.). *5 Things About Overcoming Adversity That Athletes Can Teach Entrepreneurs*. Athlete Network.

When used correctly, willpower will help you to enhance your time as a student-athlete.

You know what they say: "When the going gets tough, the tough get going."

So, use your willpower to help get you going and grow.

CHAPTER 6

WILLING TO SACRIFICE

The good and the great are separated by their willingness to sacrifice.

—KAREEM ABDUL-JABBAR, SIX-TIME NBA MVP[37]

Willpower doesn't only include overcoming challenges.

Along with facing adversity, student-athletes at the collegiate level must make sacrifices.

Many people do not realize this fact, because college athletics is typically portrayed glamorously by the media. But do not let what you see on TV fool you: it's a constant grind

---

37 BrainyQuote. (n.d.). *Kareem Abdul-Jabbar Quotes.*

that requires immense daily effort. The media doesn't often illustrate this reality.

Demonstrating willpower during these times will help you to further build and develop your character.

As athletes, we grow up making sacrifices.

These sacrifices probably started at a young age, when you first started to become serious about your sport. I can remember not being able to go to sleepovers with my friends or missing some of my best friends' graduation parties in high school because I had a softball game or was on the road headed to a tournament.

At first, making a sacrifice isn't a good feeling.

To put it simply, you get FOMO (fear of missing out).

You feel guilty and never know if you made the right decision. But after continuing to sacrifice different things, you become accustomed to the process and don't think twice about it. The decision becomes easy because you make sacrifices that bring you closer to reaching your goals.

Each sacrifice you make has a purpose. You aren't just doing it for no reason.

Sacrificing is similar to the principle of opportunity cost that you probably learned in high school economics: a benefit, profit, or value of something that must be given up to acquire something else.

Personally, I gave up the sleepovers and hangout sessions with friends to achieve my dream of playing college softball. Of course, I valued the time with my friends, but I knew what I needed to do to reach my goal.

* * *

All student-athletes have to make a sacrifice of some sort.

Kendall Spencer is a former student-athlete who knows and understands the art of willpower and sacrificing all too well.

I consider Kendall the ideal student-athlete, one everyone should try to emulate in some way, shape, or form. He was a track and field athlete at the University of New Mexico.

Did I mention that he is a national champion in the long jump? That national title wasn't attained without making several sacrifices and being a disciplined student-athlete.

On top of being a national champion, Kendall excelled in the classroom and had many leadership opportunities that helped him to grow personally and professionally. He worked his way up into a national leadership role for the NCAA Student-Athlete Advisory Committee (SAAC) and became the first student-athlete to ever sit on the board of directors for the NCAA.

At the University of New Mexico, Kendall majored in psychology with minors in both sociology and business. Following graduation, he attended the University of Massachusetts Amherst to study neuroscience but later discovered his real passion was in law. Kendall is now a law student at Georgetown University while training for the 2020 Olympic Trials.

To achieve his many athletic and academic successes, Kendall had to work hard to juggle school, track, and work successfully. When I asked Kendall what a typical day was like for him as a student-athlete, he broke down his hectic, jam-packed schedule for me.

Starting at 6 a.m., he would wake up, hit the weight room, and then make his way to his first class of the day, which started at 8 a.m. The rest of his classes followed and would wrap up around noon. Then, around 1 p.m., Kendall would head down to the training room before practice, which started at 1:30 p.m. After two to three hours of practice, he would go lift for a second session. After round two of lifting, Kendall would do any necessary rehab and preventive measures, which took him until 6 p.m.

In the evenings, Kendall would go to the research lab to finish up a project he was working on at that time until 9 p.m. or so. During his first two years at the University of New Mexico, he actually worked as a crisis counselor and also as a behavior therapist, both of which provided him caseloads of children to work with. With these two jobs in the mix, Kendall would not get home until around 11 p.m.

Then he would go to bed, get up, and do it all again.

As you can tell, Kendall had hardly any free time throughout his day. He barely even had time to eat. He did experience some perks, however. "My schedule kept me out of trouble and it really filtered out all the people that didn't need to be in my life," Kendall commented.

Having such a demanding schedule caused Kendall to make sacrifices, such as missing out on parties or spending less time with friends. He noted how there was one single weekday in college when he and his teammates went out during the week, and it was on Tuesdays, for twenty-five-cent wings. Aside from that, they did not venture out during the week, unlike typical college students.

Kendall put his student-athlete lifestyle into perspective: "So you have a pie. You have sleep, you have your social life, and then you have your academic life. You get two small slices and a bigger sliver of something else. You can't have your cake and eat it too."

Being able to make sacrifices requires discipline, something Kendall noted as a necessary skill for *all* student-athletes.

Keeping yourself disciplined and focused on your goals allows you to make the tough sacrifices. Having a strong discipline allowed Kendall to keep a good balance between being a student and an athlete.

"Truth be told, anybody can get up and go to practice. Anybody can get up and go to class. But to be able to do both of those things simultaneously and do them well, that's where it becomes hard. In order to do that, you have to be disciplined," he said.

* * *

The pie analogy is something that college students, in general, use a lot to describe their lives and the typical struggles associated with college.

The analogy that I see most when browsing social media is the triangle. At each point of the triangle is an aspect of a college student's life.

- Good Grades,
- Social Life,
- Enough Sleep.

In the center of the triangle, it says choose two.[38]

If you follow what the image says, you have good grades and a social life, good grades and enough sleep, or a social life and enough sleep.

Having a job is not even accounted for in the triangle.

Now imagine throwing athletics into the mix as well.

It does not quite balance out.

For me, my two choices varied depending on whether it was softball season and on my class workload for the week.

Out of season, I focused on good grades and social life, because once I was in season, my social life went away. When I say social life, I am referring to my different extracurriculars, such as clubs and student organizations, as well as spending time with friends.

---

38   Arvin, M. (2012). *College Triangle*. WordPress.

During softball season, my focus shifted from social life to enough sleep. My grades I still held as a top priority. I had to cut back on my extracurriculars because of practices, games, and schoolwork.

There is simply no easy way to juggle being a student-athlete.

* * *

Athletic administrators at all colleges recognize how challenging it can be to balance being a student-athlete. Dan Bartholomae, deputy director for capital projects and internal operations at Oregon State University, has experience helping student-athletes keep their crazy schedules and lives in balance.

Although Dan was not a student-athlete at Indiana University, he played soccer up through high school and always enjoyed being in a sports environment. One of his favorite aspects of his job is the opportunity to work alongside coaches and athletes to help them in any way he can.

While talking with Dan, I expressed how challenging it can be to keep the schedule of a student-athlete balanced at all levels of play. Dan sees this struggle as one of the most difficult aspects of student-athlete development in college athletics, but especially at the Division I level.

"You've got your workouts, you've got your academic schedule, and you've got your extracurriculars. How do you balance all of these things and still focus to be the best in all of these areas?" Dan explained.

This problem relates back to the triangle image, picking two areas to focus on and excel in.

In the case of a student-athlete, their sport is always going to be one of their two priorities.

* * *

As a student-athlete, I have experienced stress with time demands and missing class, just like Dan mentioned.

When softball was in season, I typically woke up around 5:30 a.m. and went to bed around midnight. Even though I was awake for over eighteen hours, I never got as much accomplished during a day as I hoped for. This lifestyle became taxing—not only mentally, but also on my body.

From an academic standpoint, I was constantly missing class every spring semester.

With a sport such as softball, the weather is the main determinant of whether games get played. During my sophomore year, I missed fifteen accounting classes and was responsible for making up all the material I missed during class. Thus, my stress from missing class translated into time demand stress because I had no idea when or how I was supposed to get my classwork done. Despite the stress, I continued to push through because I was willing to make those sacrifices and get the work done.

You need self-control and discipline to make sacrifices.

This idea is another component of Wooden's Pyramid of Success. As Wooden said, "Practice self-discipline and keep emotions under control. Good judgment and common sense are essential."[39]

When you make a sacrifice, nothing should be a rash decision. Although our emotions may sometimes try to get the best of us, we have to put them aside when making sacrifices. Now, I am not talking about positive emotions such as passion or joy; I am talking about the ones that cause us to act rashly, such as anger and disappointment.

Like I mentioned before, athletes are very passionate people.

"This characteristic within the Pyramid of Success addresses the importance of controlling yourself in all areas—avoiding

---

39   Coach John Wooden. (2019). *Pyramid of Success - Coach John Wooden.*

temptations, avoiding emotionalism, avoiding peaks and valleys of effort," Wooden elaborated.

If you avoid temptations and your emotions, the sacrifices you make will be for good reasons.

As demonstrated, the life of a student-athlete is most certainly not easy. It takes willpower in the form of sacrifice. You have to determine what is of value to you so you can make the correct sacrifice, and doing so takes discipline.

Whether with your academics, sport, social, or professional life, sacrifices must be made. However, you must be careful not to make sacrifices that will be detrimental to your health, both physically and mentally.

Show your discipline in a useful and effective manner.

Use your time as a student-athlete to practice sacrifice and discipline to reach your goals.

WILLPOWER TAKEAWAYS:
- When the going gets tough, the tough get going.
- Adversity will help you to grow.
- Make sacrifices that will help you reach your goals.

CHAPTER 7

NERVE

Success is never final; failure is never fatal. It's courage that counts.

—JOHN WOODEN[40]

Perhaps John Wooden said it best. Success and failure are cyclical, and nothing is truly final.

Nerve is defined by dictionary.com as "firmness or courage under trying circumstances," as well as demonstrating boldness during the process.[41]

---

40 BrainyQuote. (n.d.). *John Wooden Quotes.*
41 www.dictionary.com. (n.d.). *Definition of nerving | Dictionary.com.*

Courage and nerve go hand in hand. Nerve helps you bounce back from failure and allows you to keep building off success. Nerve essentially builds upon willpower, as it takes willpower to help you demonstrate nerve and vice versa. As discussed, student-athletes constantly undergo and overcome challenges. Willpower is the underlying basis that allows you to exemplify nerve and push past obstacles you may face.

Everyone expresses nerve differently. I used hard work as an avenue to do so—which I know sounds pretty vague. In my student-athlete experience, it encompassed practicing softball, studying for classes, exercising, and communicating effectively so that my goals were known.

Student-athletes often have to demonstrate nerve in their sport, as well as in their education. They must have the courage to go out and accomplish what they want to in both of these areas simultaneously. That's tough to do, which is perhaps why **15%** of scholarship athletes quit playing their sport after a year or two, according to the *New York Times*.[42]

Now, don't get me wrong: it takes nerve to come to the realization that it is best for you to quit your sport and focus more of your attention on academics. Making that executive

---

42   Pennington, B. (2008). *It's Not an Adventure, It's a Job.* Nytimes.com.

decision is challenging. However, it takes more nerve to continue pushing on in academics and athletics together.

* * *

Believe it or not, communicating in the collegiate setting takes a lot of nerve. Nerve is typically demonstrated verbally. Think about how many people college athletes have to communicate with regularly:

- Coaches,
- Assistant Coaches,
- Teammates,
- Athletic Administrators,
- Professors,
- Classmates,
- Family.

The list goes on and on.

Communicating the same message to all these individuals simultaneously can be challenging, especially if none of them are on the same page to start with. As athletes, you are going to be pulled in a million different directions at once, so it is important to find your nerve and speak up.

* * *

This issue is something that can be initially challenging for student-athletes.

For the majority of your life, your parents probably kept you on track and served as the main people you had to communicate with. They told you exactly where and when you had somewhere to be. Now, you have to know where and when you need to be and communicate it effectively with more than seven other individuals.

The same goes for when you were in high school. Your coaches, athletic directors, teachers, and principals typically communicate with one another given that it is a smaller setting.

In college athletics, you will find more moving parts, which can, unfortunately, create separation between academics and athletics.

First and foremost, way more people work in a college athletic department than a high school one—that's a given. The same goes for the academic side, which is where the student-athlete comes into play.

"You have your coaches. You have us. You have your professors. You have your trainers. ... Everybody has to be on the same page, and everybody has to communicate," said

Heather Ryan, executive director of academic services at Duke University.

Heather has witnessed firsthand how harmful a lack of communication can be. She gave me one piece of advice to relay to student-athletes:

"**OWN** your education."

Taking **OWN**ership of something most definitely takes nerve.

At Duke, Heather's role involves helping student-athletes navigate their education so that their experience can be as tailored to them as possible. This approach is made possible by ensuring student-athletes understand that academics are a priority.

"Yes, they are student-athletes and being an athlete does take up a lot of their time," Heather acknowledged, "but they are under the understanding when they step foot on this campus that they are also students and that they're going to earn their degree."

Taking **OWN**ership of your education can be challenging. Heather commented on the crucial nature of communication when it comes to taking the reins on your education. As a student-athlete, you have many different people to make aware of your schedule. The communication all starts with the student-athlete, which is where nerve comes into play.

* * *

Unfortunately, the times of college courses do not always accommodate the crazy schedule of student-athletes. There are going to be times—many times if you play a sport with games on weekdays—where you are going to miss class. Scheduling conflicts happen more often than not. The more challenging piece of it all, however, is that some professors are more accepting of this reality than others. You definitely need nerve to have the confidence to go up to a professor who you know is not understanding of your schedule and tell them you are not going to be in class due to sport-related reasons.

Take it from me: I have had my fair share of conversations with professors who do not find a collegiate softball game on the road an acceptable excuse to miss class. You may find it intimidating to tell your professor that when you know it is going to be a problem. But you find your nerve and do it because you know you have to.

At the Division II and III levels, designated faculty members typically help when an athletic and academic scheduling conflict arises. The Division I level usually has staff members

whose job is to alert professors to athletic scheduling conflicts, just like Heather does for student-athletes at Duke.

The reverse is also true.

Especially at the Division III level, where resources are limited and academic requirements are stricter, student-athletes
will have to miss practices for class if they have a time conflict. Such outcomes are inevitable. It can be difficult to pull
yourself out of a practice to head to class. Some coaches are
better at understanding the importance of class than others.
When you have a coach who is not completely understanding
of athletes leaving to attend class, it can be terrifying to tell
them, "Hey, Coach. I have to go to class."

That takes nerve too.

You feel guilty for missing practice and you also feel as
though you're missing out. You also do not want to miss
something important at practice.

At first, I was scared that having to miss practice for class
would affect my playing time, but I eventually had to realize
that there was nothing I could do about it. There were some
classes I needed to take to graduate, which helped to paint a
bigger picture for me.

Good communication is an effective way of taking **OWN**ership of your education. The more you **OWN** your education, the more you will value it.

The easiest way to build up nerve is to develop a plan for yourself. Answer the following questions:

- What are your goals academically?

- What are your goals athletically?

- Where do you want to be when your time as a student-athlete is complete?

When you are aware of your goals, you will have an easier time finding your nerve to speak up when something interferes with achieving them.

To get to this point, though, significant understanding is required.

First and foremost, you have to focus on the requirements that are going to help you achieve your degree. Reiterating what Heather said, **OWN** your education. Within this principle comes knowing and understanding your curriculum, which is what Heather responded with when I asked her some of her best academic strategies to keep student-athletes on track to graduate.

Know your academic track like the back of your hand.

This tactic means being aware of how many credits you need to graduate, what core requirements are in your major, what number of electives you need to take, and whether you need an internship. Knowing this information will help you set your goals, which will then help you show nerve when the time is right.

* * *

Going back to John Wooden's quotation, we can easily see why nerve is important in the life of a student-athlete. If it weren't for nerve,

- How would we be able to experience success after failure?

- How would we continue to push past the challenges we are faced with as student-athletes?

- How would we be prepared to face challenges later on down the road in our career and life?

As student-athletes, we are on a rollercoaster of highs and lows. Ride the highs and build off the lows, but continue to push yourself regardless of whether you are experiencing success or failure.

To push yourself, figure out your goals and what is important to you. For me, it was playing softball to the best of my ability and graduating college, simultaneously. Playing softball in college was a goal of mine for as long as I can remember, but so was getting a college diploma. I worked hard to achieve both these goals.

Find your willpower so that you can have the nerve to speak up for what is right for you. By demonstrating nerve, you won't only be able to **OWN** your education, you'll also be able to **OWN** and take the reins on other aspects of your life too.

CHAPTER 8

NERVE TO COURAGE
TO CONFIDENCE

———

You must expect great things of yourself before you can do them.

—MICHAEL JORDAN[43]

When you think of being a student-athlete, courage probably isn't necessarily the first quality that comes to mind.

Why would being an athlete take courage?

In reality, the whole cycle of becoming an athlete takes courage. Think about it.

———

43   Goodreads.com. (n.d.). *A Quote by Michael Jordan.*

You probably started playing your first sport at a young age. You had no clue what was going on, but you continued to play because it was fun. Every time the ball came to you, you got nervous and even a little scared, but you did what you had to in order to complete the play to the best of your ability.

That's courage.

Then you became better at your sport and went to your first tryout for an all-star or travel team. You put yourself and your athletic abilities out there for people to judge.

That's courage.

Then, you immersed yourself in the college recruiting process, an even bigger stage and tryout.

That takes a lot of courage.

By definition, courage is "the ability to do something that frightens one."[44]

I am not saying that you were frightened for each of these steps, but you definitely encountered a level of uncertainty and that in itself can be scary. As athletes, you will always

44 Lexico Dictionaries | English. (n.d.). *Courage | Definition of Courage by Lexico.*

find another hurdle to overcome, some more frightening and larger than others. As student-athletes, we face even more hurdles than the average college student. But once we overcome one, we are more willing and able to overcome more.

* * *

If anyone knows about being a student-athlete and courage, it's Beth Brooke-Marciniak.

Beth, the former global vice chairwoman of public policy at Ernst & Young, became a college athlete at an exciting time. She had enormous success professionally, which is something she attributes to her impactful experience as a student-athlete.

Beth was among the first class of female athletes to have athletic scholarships available to them. Title IX had just been passed, and Beth had her eyes set on receiving a scholarship. Title IX states, "No person in the United States shall, on the basis of sex, be excluded from participation in, be denied the benefits of, or be subjected to discrimination under any education program or activity receiving Federal financial assistance."[45] Pertaining to the world of college athletics, this law applies primarily to participation and athletic scholarships.

---

45   www2.ed.gov. (2015). *Title IX and Sex Discrimination.*

Basically, Title IX requires women and men to be provided the same opportunity to participate in sports.

From a scholarship standpoint, the law necessitates that "female and male student-athletes receive athletics scholarship dollars proportional to their participation." Beth was a part of a critical group of women who helped shape college athletics for female athletes. Taking the initial step to be a part of this inaugural class took courage, especially since no women had ever had an opportunity like this before.

Growing up, Beth was a well-rounded athlete; her two main sports were softball and basketball. She admitted to me that she was actually a better softball player, but it was not yet classified as an intercollegiate sport. So, Beth took her basketball talents to Purdue University because of the athletic scholarship tied to her acceptance. Deciding to forgo her main sport for a basketball scholarship exemplifies another way Beth was courageous during her time as a student-athlete.

Beth knew she wasn't going to be a professional basketball player from the beginning. Because of this, she became very focused on her academics, starting the moment she stepped onto Purdue's campus.

"This was my future. I wasn't going to squander it," Beth said.

And she most certainly did not.

On top of being a dedicated athlete on the women's basketball team, Beth graduated first in her class at Purdue and received a top score on the CPA exam. She was one of the first successful female student-athletes on scholarship.

Beth paved the way for female collegiate student-athletes and set the standard high.

When I asked Beth if there was a pivotal moment during her student-athlete career, she talked about a valuable internship experience in New York City.

"I got away from school, I got away from sports, I got away from family and I had to go to New York, find a place to live while working for a company. I had a summer of just knocking it out of the park and finding myself in the corporate world. ... I gained confidence," she recalled.

The confidence gained from her internship translated back into her senior year at Purdue, both academically and athletically. Beth's internship paired with her student-athlete experience helped set her up for professional success after graduation.

In fact, many college athletic programs are beginning to build programs for student-athletes to help them lock in internships and prepare for their future careers. According to *The Hechinger Report*, "The Ohio State University launched a summer internship program for student-athletes, the University of Michigan invests heavily in student-athlete career development, and Arkansas State University created a robust job placement program that matches student-athletes with alumni mentors."[46]

As a student-athlete, you may find it easy to say no to opportunities that could interfere with your growth and development as an athlete, but you have to look at the bigger picture. Clearly some college athletic departments are starting to look at the bigger picture too. For Beth, the bigger picture was that she wasn't going to play basketball professionally, so she needed to find professional success elsewhere to support herself in the future.

That's exactly what she did.

Beth climbed the corporate ladder, eventually working her way up to achieving accolades such as being recognized seven times by *Forbes Magazine* as one of the World's 100 Most Powerful Women. She attributes every bit of her success to her college athletic experience. Beth believes that her

---

46 Blue, K. and Criag, R. (2019). *College athletes beating the odds in career quest.* The Hechinger Report.

experience as a student-athlete provided her a leg up on others in her industry and allowed her to prove herself.

"As an athlete, you want the ball with two seconds to go, and in business, you want the responsibility. You're the one who steps up. You don't step back and that all comes from an athletic background," Beth encouraged.

Stepping up, as Beth mentions, essentially encompasses almost all that this book has discussed thus far:

- Willpower,
- Nerve,
- Courage.

When I talked with Beth, I was a graduating senior headed into the workforce. I was eager to know what advice Beth could offer, given her athletic and professional success.

To put it simply, confidence is key. Beth advised:

Be really confident in what you have that no one else has, which is leadership talent. You know the recipe for success because you have proven it day in and day out of your sporting career. That recipe for success, meaning preparation and hard work, you know, outworking the other person and being focused on the ultimate goal ... I mean, all of those things translate very naturally into business. You never walk into a meeting unprepared and you would never go into a game without having studied game film. You just translate all those things you learned on the field into your business environment. The leg up you have on every other non-athlete is that you know the recipe for winning.

From an athletic perspective, *HuffPost News* recognized confidence as "the single most important mental factor in sports."[47] This notion is one coaches preach to their athletes every day.

"Be confident."

How many times have we heard it?

We are most confident when we are performing at our best, naturally. That idea goes for athletics and academics. The trick is continuing to remain confident in your abilities and in yourself regardless of what your performance outcome is.

That's a challenge in itself. You need courage to do that.

* * *

---

47 Taylor, D. (2011). *Confidence Matters for Athletes*. Huffpost.com.

Confidence and courage go hand in hand.

Let's go back to the definition of courage: "the ability to do something that frightens one."

Overcoming something that scares you requires some sort of confidence. Luckily for us, our designated sports have taught us to be confident in ourselves and to be courageous on various occasions. Both are qualities you have to grasp quickly if you want to be successful athletically and professionally.

Confidence also features on John Wooden's Pyramid of Success. Within the pyramid it says, "Respect without fear. May come from being prepared and keeping all things in proper perspective."[48] This statement is true, but what Wooden described in his book on leadership speaks volumes. "Confidence cannot be grafted on artificially. True abiding confidence is earned through tenaciously pursuing and attaining those assets that allow you to reach your own level of competency; that is, excellence," he said.[49]

Essentially, the confidence you have in yourself has to be genuine and real or else it won't help you.

---

48 Coach John Wooden. (2019). *Pyramid of Success - Coach John Wooden*.
49 Coachwooden.com. (2019). *Official Site of Coach Wooden*.

Confidence can be a tough skill to emulate, especially with the highs and lows of sports. I know that it is a trait that comes and goes for me.

Beth Brooke-Marciniak said she would hire student-athletes all day if she could, because she knows that they know how to be confident, not only in themselves but also in teammates, on and off the field. Once you transition into your career, your coworkers become your teammates. Beth also knows that student-athletes know how to be leaders and possess the courage to do so.

To put it simply:

Demonstrate nerve.

Be confident in yourself.

Have the courage to do what others can't.

NERVE TAKEAWAYS:

- Discover your goals and use your nerve to drive you.
- Take **OWN**ership of what is yours.
- Find your confidence.

CHAPTER 9

INTROSPECTION

———

After thorough reflection, I realized that my desire to achieve
my goals in this sport outweighed my self-doubt. This perse-
verance has helped me to be successful not only in gymnastics
but in my non-athletic life as well.

—JONATHAN HORTON, TWO-TIME OLYMPIC

GYMNAST AND BRONZE MEDALIST[50]

The quotation above resonates with me for several reasons.

First, it depicts an Olympian admitting he has self-doubt,
proving that he is just like the rest of us. Second, Horton
adds that perseverance has allowed him to find success both

———

50   A-Z Quotes. (n.d.). *Jonathan Horton Quote.*

inside and outside of gymnastics, which alludes to the idea that he uses what his sport has taught him in his life outside of it. Lastly, he mentions reflection.

The college I attended, John Carroll University, is a Jesuit school. Jesuits are a sector of the Roman Catholic Church mostly known for doing missionary work. They are also very well known for their education system, which focuses on creating well-rounded individuals and future leaders.

Up until attending college, I had only gone to public school. Once I got to college, my school kept stressing the importance of reflection. I am not going to lie; I kind of thought it was B.S. at first because I had never really done it on a personal level. It wasn't until one of my professors strongly encouraged me to do it as a part of my coursework that I discovered and found the value in it.

Reflecting, on essentially anything, can help you learn and discover different things about yourself from your experiences. It has helped me to see what I have done well and also what I can improve on. Reflection also allows you to look at an experience from a slightly different perspective once it is over.

This concept is similar to introspection, which is the process of examining, observing, or reflecting on yourself. The "I" in **OWN IT.**

You can easily become blinded by everything going on around you. As student-athletes, we are pulled in a thousand different directions and must be able to handle whatever is thrown our way. Taking the time to reflect, gain perspective, and understand the world around you will help you to improve yourself as a student, an athlete, and a professional.

* * *

Jamie Mullin, the senior associate director of athletics at Syracuse University, used reflection as a tool to help him discover what exactly he wanted to do for the rest of his life. As a football student-athlete at Northern Michigan University, a Division II institution, Jamie found himself in a competitive environment, which helped him grow.

In high school, Jamie was not the most motivated student. Once he stepped onto Northern Michigan University's campus, however, he began to take a lot of pride in many areas in his life. This new mindset eventually became apparent when he graduated magna cum laude, something he would have never thought feasible while in high school. But, by stepping back and introspecting about himself and his future goals, Jamie was able to make the most of his student-athlete experience to determine his professional career path.

"I competed hard in the classroom and, upon reflection, I discovered that athletics really helped to round me out as a person," Jamie explained. "When you look at what inter-collegiate athletic programs are trying to do in the sense of helping student-athletes develop as a person, it's pretty special. So, as I was thinking, I want to be a part of this because it transformed me personally."

Personally, I had a slightly different experience.

In high school, I always held academics as a top priority and was a motivated student. However, once I got to college, my priorities shifted, not because I was no longer motivated—I definitely still was. Softball just became the only thing that motivated me. I had tunnel vision on earning my position on the softball team. This goal was probably the theme of my freshman year.

I was constantly focused on softball.

At the time, I did not find anything wrong with that, but you know what they say: hindsight is 20/20. Now, I still realize that there is nothing wrong with fully focusing on your sport, but there is more to your student-athlete experience than just your sport.

The difference in experience between my freshman and sophomore years was because of the summer in between them. I had the opportunity to do some serious personal reflecting, which helped me to discover that I wasn't as happy as I could be—because I was so consumed by softball:

- It was all I talked about.
- It was all I focused on.
- It was all I did.

For my own personal reasons, I needed to become involved in more outside of my sport. I would not have come to this realization if I did not take the time to engage in introspection. Doing so allowed me to become motivated in several areas that I was not during my freshman year.

* * *

I also had the pleasure of speaking with Amanda Gray, associate athletic director for football compliance at Clemson University. Amanda not only provided excellent insight on what the 2019 National Champions go through on a daily basis but also on her role as an administrator for the team.

During our conversation, we kept circling back to the extensive time demands of student-athletes.

And I mean *extensive* time demands.

As difficult as it may be, you will come across a time when you will need to step back, take it all in, and become more aware of your surroundings. Having these extensive time demands makes it challenging to keep the balance between student and athlete.

"I don't want to say it's impossible, but..." Amanda said, in reference to balancing student and athlete.

At the Division II and III levels, juggling the two is slightly more manageable. But at the Division I level and within certain sports, the challenge is much more prevalent.

Take Division I football for example, specifically Clemson's program. Amanda shared with me how the football student-athletes have their own dining hall, weight room, and study areas within the Allen N. Reeves Football Complex. This facility gives the athletes almost everything they need under one roof to help make it easier for them to accomplish all they need to in one day.

Although this state-of-the-art facility is put to good use and allows the team to become close, it tends to seclude the football athletes from other student-athletes on campus. This isolation can make it more difficult to achieve balance. Even though the facility has study areas for the student-athletes, players may still feel like they are at football even while working on coursework. As a result, players may feel like they never get away from football, especially while they are in season.

Most top-tier Division I programs have a facility similar to Clemson's.

* * *

Now, I am definitely not comparing my experience as a student-athlete to that of a Clemson football player. Only a small fraction of student-athletes have an experience like that. Playing football for a program that is consistently ranked one or two in the college football standings requires serious commitment and may not allow you to branch out as much as you would like, but you can find feasible ways to spread your horizons. Through my personal reflection, I discovered that I needed to venture out beyond my sport.

Now, I realize that some student-athletes only need their sport to be happy, and their approach is perfectly fine. My point is that you have to uncover what is best for you, which may differ from what is best for someone else. Thus, you must conduct a personal reflection to discover how you can best suit yourself and your situation.

The beautiful thing about introspection is that you can do it in a number of different ways. There is no one right way to do it. For me, I reflected right before bed. No matter how busy I was that day or the next, I always took a couple of minutes for myself. Setting aside this time every night to reflect on what I did well that day and what I needed to improve on helped me to get into a positive mindset for the following day. It also allowed me to discover what I valued.

Someone else, meanwhile, might like to introspect during their walk to class in the morning.

Like I said, there is no right or wrong way to do it.

At the Division II and III levels, the time demands are consuming, but more opportunities exist to find a better balance of student and athlete, just like I was able to find. John Carroll University provided me with the opportunity to play softball while also involving myself in several different extracurriculars on campus. However, with that said, I couldn't get involved in as many extracurriculars as I would have liked.

I had to make sacrifices. I had to turn down involvement in other activities because I simply could not handle more. Through introspection, I realized that I simply couldn't take on more. I learned when to say no, especially when I knew I couldn't afford more on my plate. I decided exactly what sacrifices to make through personal reflection, which allowed me to uncover what was most important to me.

* * *

As a professional, Amanda Gray also had to have moments of introspection to figure out how she could be better for Clemson student-athletes.

Amanda always worked in compliance, but about a year and a half ago she shifted over to strictly working with the Clemson football team. Athletic compliance involves keeping student-athletes and coaches within the framework of the NCAA. Essentially, Amanda has to keep over 100 student-athletes NCAA eligible.

Working with the Clemson football staff and football student-athletes, Amanda educates them on several complicated rules and regulations. The most challenging aspect of her job is enforcing penalties for broken rules. To make this challenging aspect of her job a little easier, Amanda likes to be a relational administrator.

"I like to go down and have breakfast and lunch with our student-athletes, so they see me on a personal level, as opposed to someone that stands up in front of them three times a year and talks at them. I like my cordial relationship with them so when things do go wrong it's more than just like I'm coming in to get them in trouble and they know that they can come to me," Amanda said.

In order to get on a personal level with her student-athletes, Amanda reflected on her job description and wanted to find a way for herself to somewhat step into the athletes' shoes. That's why she goes to breakfast and lunch with the team. That's why she gets up early for some of their morning practices. She sees the daily grind that the Clemson student-athletes go through and tries to relate to them in any way she can. Amanda wants to be as visible to them as she can be, and she made this decision through reflection and introspection on a professional level.

* * *

As you can see, the act of introspection is one you can apply to your personal, collegiate, and professional life. It's not about focusing or dwelling on the past. It's all about making improvements to your future.

Circling back to Jonathan Horton's quotation, reflect to find ways to be successful both inside and outside of your sport.

CHAPTER 10

REFLECTING ON THE PRIVILEGE

———

What makes something special is not just what you have to gain, but what you feel there is to lose.

—ANDRE AGASSI, PROFESSIONAL TENNIS PLAYER
AND EIGHT-TIME GRAND SLAM WINNER[51]

The things you will discover when you introspect will open your eyes and help you come to several realizations. You'll have new perspectives on things that you have known and understood your whole life.

———

51 Goodreads.com. (n.d.). *A quote by Andre Agassi.*

When I would reflect in college, it helped me realize how lucky I was to have the opportunity to play the sport I loved collegiately. Although softball had been a huge part of my life for at least fifteen years, I still complained about it and took it for granted a lot.

Every year, **1 in every 14** high school athletes embark on the journey of taking their athletic career to the collegiate level.[52]

That's **7%**.

This ratio represents all levels of intercollegiate athletics.

From there, the number of student-athletes who stick to playing their sport through all four years of college is quite small.

Every year, **33%** of that **7%** quit playing college athletics.[53]

Thus being a college athlete is a privilege and certainly something special.

Tommy Zagorski understands this concept quite well. The offensive coordinator for the University of Akron football

---

52 NCAA.org - The Official Site of the NCAA. (n.d.). *Student-Athletes.*
53 Corona, Z. (2014). 36 Reasons Why 33% of College Athletes Quit, Get Cut or Get Asked To Leave!. [Blog] *BeRecruited.*

team has had some experiences that make him value his time as a student-athlete now more than ever.

* * *

Growing up, Tommy was a multi-sport athlete. When the time came for him to choose one to focus on and take to the next level, he decided on football. Although it wasn't the sport he was best at, his high school football team's success motivated him to continue on with the sport. "It just became the sport that I embraced and loved," Tommy recalled.

Tommy decided to take his football career to the next level at Case Western Reserve University. Case Western, esteemed for its academics, was not known for its football team at the time.

That all changed once Tommy stepped onto the urban campus.

"A culture shock" is how Tommy initially described his college football experience during his freshman year. Tommy can recall walking into the locker room for his first-ever college football game and seeing a player reading a physics book.

Is this the way we prepare for games? he thought to himself in confusion.

"When you walk into a facility here, your whole mindset should be football. Your mind should be on the whole sport itself and nothing else. Football should be your opportunity to escape academics and anything else on your mind," Tommy said.

A majority of the Case Western football team viewed football as just a hobby, not a passion like Tommy did.

After some serious thought and introspection, Tommy knew the collegiate program needed a major change. He came from a high school team where everyone lived and breathed football. To see this change through, Tommy sat down with some of his coaches, and they began to implement some initial adjustments.

Tommy served as the catalyst for an impactful change.

"Every player in the program helped with recruiting. Every player in the program wanted to make sure that we had the best," Tommy described.

After adopting this mindset and attitude, the drastic advancements within the team were eminent—and not only in the team, but also in people outside of the program. The Case Western football team began winning the majority of their games and eventually climbed their way up to being a top-ten team by Tommy's senior year.

Looking back on his team's evolution, "It was amazing to see a community that wasn't a football community be graced with victory and celebration. We had a lot of people that started coming to games that probably never would have and we were fortunate for that," Tommy said. The Case Western Reserve University football team finally viewed football as a privilege, not a hobby.

Here is an instance where previous experiences and introspection can be used for positive change.

* * *

As a student-athlete, with the pressure of athletics and academics, it can be easy to get caught up in multitasking, such as studying for physics in the locker room, like Tommy experienced. But once the team was able to recognize their true potential as football players and focus on that, the results were encouraging. Think about the player who was used to reading his physics book prior to a game inside the locker room. He had to reflect on himself to change the way he operated for the greater good of the team.

In addition, Tommy had a more personal experience that required some serious thought and reflection. From this challenge, Tommy developed an even deeper appreciation for football and the privilege that being a student-athlete is.

The transition between his junior and senior years of college is one Tommy will never forget.

Throughout college, Tommy had to work in order to afford his top-notch education.

Not just one job.

Two jobs during the school year and three jobs during the summer.

Working this much during the summer did not leave Tommy with enough time to do his football workouts before his junior year, which resulted in him pulling his hamstring when he returned to camp. He came back a week later from his hamstring injury only to experience a high ankle sprain, which turned out to be a broken ankle.

Tommy ended up having to sit out the rest of his junior season.

Spring semester during his junior year, Tommy realized he did not have enough money to attend school, forcing him to drop out for a period of time.

Three jobs during the summer, and he still had drop out for financial reasons.

This setback was simply devastating for him, considering it was technically the spring football season of Tommy's senior year. A season that was supposed to be Tommy's best one yet.

He was a guy everyone on the team looked up to—not to mention, he was also a four-year captain of the team.

In order to get back to Case Western and to his football team, Tommy needed to work. "I dropped out of school and got a job working construction here in northeast Ohio. Then in the evenings, to keep myself in a competitive nature, I started to coach middle school track," Tommy explained.

Every penny that Tommy earned went right back into his education fund to get him back to Case Western Reserve University. Fortunately, he was able to enroll in the fall after taking a whole semester off.

After working endless days and nights to help him get back into the university, another setback occurs.

Case Western partnered with the University of Pittsburgh for a concussion study that Tommy willingly participated in. He took the baseline test and his scores were surprisingly awful.

"I get my results back, and they say, 'This guy has the brain of a 45-year-old boxer,'" Tommy recounted.

Tommy lost the opportunity to play on the field next to the guys he came into Case Western Reserve University with because he did not get cleared to play due to his baseline results.

Everything he had worked so hard for was taken away in a matter of minutes.

* * *

Fast-forward seven weeks into what would have been his senior football season, it was discovered that Tommy actually took the baseline concussion test incorrectly.

He was cleared to play.

He could have been playing his senior season this whole time.

"Would you rather play three games or would you rather have the opportunity to play your true senior year?" his coach asked him.

Tommy figured since he was going to be enrolled again in school anyway, he might as well wait to make the following season his final one. He took the time that he was not playing and became a student coach, which provided him with a whole new perspective on the game of football.

When he came back for his real senior season the follow-ing fall, he had so much more knowledge about the game because of his coaching experience. He was ready to have a great senior season.

The ups and downs that Tommy went through as a stu-dent-athlete at Case Western Reserve University are unimag-inable. What he experienced with his financial problems, injuries, and alleged concussion taught him that playing a sport and being a student-athlete is a privilege, a mantra he continues to preach to his football players at the University of Akron.

But let's talk about the decision he had to come to, deciding to forgo his senior season with the guys he started his stu-dent-athlete experience with. At the time, that choice was probably the biggest one Tommy ever had to make. He knew when he had to stop and wait for his next opportunity. Com-ing to this conclusion required Tommy to stop, reflect, and figure out what was important to him.

* * *

For student-athletes, it is easy to go through the motions.

It can also be easy to take our sport for granted.

We don't realize in the moment that what we are doing is special. Finding time to introspect more can help you recognize the privilege that is right in front of you. You have to remember that you only get four years of opportunity to play your sport at the collegiate level. I cannot emphasize enough how quickly it goes.

Don't blink.

We are a part of the minuscule 7% that made it this far.

The path you chose—being a student-athlete—is truly a privilege.

CHAPTER 11

INTROSPECT TO CONNECT

—

Passion is what makes life interesting, what ignites our soul, fuels our love and carries our friendships, stimulates our intellect, and pushes our limits.

—PAT TILLMAN, FORMER NFL PLAYER WHO LEFT
SPORTS TO ENLIST IN THE U.S. ARMY POST 9/11[54]

So, after you introspect, what do you do next?

Well, many options can follow, all based on the findings of your personal reflection:

54 Wild Child Sports. (n.d.). *Sports Quotes - 10 Quotes Every Athlete Must Read - Wild Child Sports.*

- You might discover your strengths and weaknesses.
- You might finalize your goals.
- You may even uncover your true passions.

As student-athletes, we know how to demonstrate passion because we regularly have to. If you weren't passionate about your sport, you definitely would not be playing it at the collegiate level. You can't do something well if you aren't passionate about it.

Your passion helps to motivate you. Introspecting helps you to determine exactly what motivates you best.

Odds are you probably have passions outside of your sport as well.

The opportunity to be a college athlete is unique, something I wish I recognized earlier on in my college career. You can major in something you are passionate about and continue to play the sport you love. You have two unique opportunities right there alone.

And, if you're lucky, you might have the opportunity to combine both.

That scenario is exactly what happened for Jenna Lilley, a former standout softball player at the University of Oregon.

* * *

During her time at the University of Oregon, Jenna made the most out of her college experience.

She was a four-year starter at third base and helped her team compete for a national championship on an annual basis. Individually, her softball talents have been recognized at the national level. On the academic side of things, Jenna majored in sociology and paired it with a minor in psychology. When she originally determined her academic path as an underclassman, she had no idea that she would eventually be able to combine both her academic and athletic passions.

When Jenna was a senior at Oregon, she became a member of the honors sociology program, which provided her with a mandatory yearlong research project. She decided to conduct her research project on student-athletes and mental health, and specifically examined anxiety and depression among young athletes.

Through introspection into both her academic and athletic passions, she found a way to focus on both. Depression in athletes has been a recent hot button topic in the sports industry. Similar to how more people are experiencing depression from social media, athletes tend to experience depression from trying to be perfect.

Jenna's findings from her research were interesting and slightly different than she originally anticipated:

I thought athletes would be more prone to these mental health concerns, but part of what I found is that we have more protective factors than non-athletes do. For starters, we have built-in exercise, which is a major protective factor against mental health issues. We have built-in support systems from the day we step on campus. We also have a lot more structure when it comes to academics and scheduling. We also tend to have better sleep schedules. So, there are all these things that can actually help student-athletes, although it does not make them immune.

While Jenna was discussing the results of her study, I could hear the excitement and genuine enthusiasm in her voice, which truly demonstrated her ability to combine her academic passion with her athletic passion.

She inspired me to find a way to do the same.

* * *

Being a student-athlete also offered Jenna some unique opportunities outside the classroom; these allowed Jenna to have more experiences, so she could reflect and discover new passions.

Through Oregon's softball team, Jenna traveled with her team during winter break to New Zealand, where they played eight games as a part of a foreign tour. This trip exposed Jenna to a new culture and country she was unfamiliar with, which helped to open her eyes to new perspectives.

Jenna also had another abroad opportunity through the Oregon athletic department. She, and eighteen other student-athletes, traveled to Canaza, Panama, through the Courts for Kids program. Courts for Kids is a nonprofit organization that began in 2007; it builds basketball courts for communities in need throughout various countries. This trip had a positive impact on Jenna and was one that she described as the most memorable during her time as a student-athlete.

While introspecting, Jenna uncovered her passion for doing service. She may not have realized this aspect of herself if she weren't a student-athlete.

Another way Jenna was able to combine her passions.

And it doesn't stop there: Jenna also served as a committee member within her athletic department's Student-Athlete Advisory Committee (SAAC). Through SAAC, Jenna was provided with opportunities to volunteer within the community and be involved in the athletic initiative Be Oregon, which focuses on diversity and inclusion within athletics at the university. This initiative again helped to connect her sociology major to her passion for athletics.

* * *

For a student-athlete, being a member of your school's SAAC is a great way to become more involved within your athletic department, but also on campus. The NCAA states that the mission of SAAC "is to enhance the total student-athlete experience by promoting opportunity, protecting student-athlete welfare and fostering a positive student-athlete image."[55] Having a hand in that mission is important and being involved with SAAC can open other doors for you as well—at the university level, the conference level, and the national level.

I became a committee member of SAAC at the end of my freshman year and I was able to learn a lot about the student-athlete experience, as well as about college athletics as a whole. Just like Jenna, I also had numerous opportunities to volunteer through SAAC, which I thoroughly enjoyed. Every year we planned a week where we would fundraise for pediatric cancer, specifically for the Max Cure Foundation, an organization the helps the families of pediatric cancer patients.

---

55   NCAA.org - The Official Site of the NCAA. (n.d.). *NCAA Student-Athlete Advisory Committees (SAACs).*

From doing this work, I was able to discover my passion for fundraising, helping others, and working in the community.

Extracurriculars, in general, are an important part of the college experience, regardless of whether you're an athlete. It's all about developing yourself, and some people use their passions as an easy way to do so. The awesome thing about college is that it has something for everyone, and I truly mean that. Anything that you're interested in—an organization for it exists. If one doesn't exist, you can start your own.

Given Jenna's success academically and athletically, I naturally had to ask her what tips she had for student-athletes to help them make the most out of their time.

Jenna started by explaining how being a student-athlete is an extraordinary experience and one that gives you a lot of unique resources that may not be available to the general student population. She emphasized the importance of taking advantage of these resources.

Jenna followed by saying, "All of the opportunities you're given, make the most of them. I got to hear a lot of cool speakers and was able to make connections with people in the sports world."

The point is:

- Introspect to help you discover what your passions are.
- See how you can combine them.
- Use your passions as a way to motivate you.

I noticed when reflecting that I performed better on the softball field when I was happier with what I was doing off the field—when I was a part of extracurriculars that I was passionate about. There's a trickle-down effect.

The inner connections you are able to make through reflection are so important; they will help you enhance your student-athlete experience.

Then, introspecting on those connections will transform your student-athlete experience.

INTROSPECTION TAKEAWAYS:
- Reflecting is useful in helping to make self-improvements.
- Don't take your privileges for granted.
- Find ways to connect your passions.

CHAPTER 12

TEAMWORK

———

Talent wins games, but teamwork and intelligence win championships.

—MICHAEL JORDAN[56]

To round it all out, the final letter in **OWN IT** represents teamwork.

How many times have you heard the corny saying: "Teamwork makes the dream work"?

Many times, if I had to take a guess. The saying gets tossed around all the time.

———

56 Freeland, G. (2018). *Talent Wins Games, Teamwork Wins Championships.* Forbes.com.

What if I told you that this motto holds more meaning than you may think?

Well, it does.

Unfortunately, because we hear it all the time, the heavy meaning of this saying has been diminished.

In a team environment, everyone has a role that serves a specific purpose, regardless of what type of team it is. But, on a sports team, these roles can be very specific and designated.

My softball coach would share two stories in particular with our team at the beginning of every season to prep us for preseason that reflects this concept perfectly.

* * *

The first story is one by Don Yaeger.

Swen Nater, a native of Holland, grew up to be 6 feet, 11 inches tall. His height caused him to be "gangly and awkward," and because of this, he didn't make his high school basketball team until senior year. Nater decided not to go to college and found a job as a mechanic. A local community college basketball coach came to the garage he was working at to get his car fixed and instantly noticed Nater's height. He convinced Nater to give basketball another chance.

Nater went on to become one of the best junior-college basketball players in the country.

When Nater had two years of eligibility left collegiately, he began to get offers from smaller schools to be their star player. Nater's coach thought he could go bigger and reached out to John Wooden, the head coach of the UCLA basketball team.

At the time, the UCLA Bruins were in the middle of one of the greatest dynasties in sports. Nater's coach said, "Coach, next year you have a guy coming in that everybody in America believes will be the greatest player to ever play college basketball." He was referring to 7-foot-tall Bill Walton. He continued, "The next biggest guy you have on your team is 6-foot-9 inches tall. In practice, Bill Walton is not going to get better every day because he's not going to have any competition. ... Give my guy a chance."

The idea here is that we get better when we are surrounded by better people, which made sense to Wooden. He offered Nater his last remaining scholarship on the UCLA men's basketball team. Wooden told Nater, "I am going to make you two promises. One, you'll probably never ever get off of the bench. But two, you're going to get a chance every day to practice against the best player in America, and I promise you, the best coaches in America are going to work with you every day."

Nater accepted the scholarship and Wooden stuck to his promise. No surprise there.

Approaching his senior year, Bill Walton was poised to be the number-one pick in the draft, as anticipated by many.

A question that Walton kept getting was "Who was the best center you played against all year long?" Walton glanced down the practice court and said, "That guy down there is the best center I've ever played against. Swen Nater." From working with Walton, Nater's basketball skills improved significantly.

In fact, the improvements were so major that he became the first player in history to never start a college basketball game and be selected in the first round of the NBA draft.

Swen Nater played twelve seasons in the NBA.[57]

* * *

You are where you are for a reason, and everyone serves a purpose.

---

57 Leading Essentially. (2018). *The Story of Bill and Swen.*

In Nater's case, he knew he was there strictly to make Bill Walton better. In spite of this duty, Nater improved his skills every day from this opportunity. Nater fulfilled his role to his fullest potential for the greater good of the team. That was his sole purpose for being on the UCLA men's basketball team.

Knowing your role and purpose is a lesson Michelle Morgan, senior director of varsity athletics and recreation at John Carroll University, learned from her student-athlete experience.

Michelle played for the women's hockey team at the University of St. Thomas in St. Paul, Minnesota, for all four years. During her time there, she experienced her fair share of ups and downs with the sport. One down for Michelle was when she blew out her knee during her freshman year. She had to have reconstructive surgery and was unable to skate for at least six months.

This created a difficult decision for Michelle: was it time for her to hang up the skates or would she work to recover to make her return?

She was not ready to give up the sport she loved because she knew one of her purposes in life was to play hockey.

When I asked Michelle what she learned from being a student-athlete, she told me this: "Being a student-athlete taught me the power of a purpose and knowing your role. Every person's role on a team is important whether you're a starter or whether you're a team manager."

This ties into the second story that my coach tells my team.

* * *

Ithaca College had one of the best softball programs in the nation during the early 2000s. The team had a lot of depth and was very talented, but what separated it from every other team in the country one year was the dedication of a senior.

In 2002, senior outfielder Sarah was ready and excited to begin her final year of her career. She played some her sophomore year, started the majority of games her junior year, and was prepared to take on the full starting role during her senior year. Sarah never expected to lose her starting position to a freshman halfway through the season. Coach Pallozzi had a discussion with Sarah, emphasizing how important her leadership was, how valuable her knowledge of the game was, and how if she truly loved this program, she would put it first.

At this point in time, Ithaca College had a real chance to get to the College World Series. Sarah accepted her new role because she knew it was what was best for the team.

Let's fast-forward twenty-seven games later to the if-necessary game of the College World Series.

Whoever won this game would be crowned the Division III NCAA National Champion. Sarah was on the bench assuming her new role as a leader. The energy in the ballpark was out of control, and the game was close. Through the first five innings, no one had scored. That all changed in the top of the sixth inning when the fourth batter hit a single down the left-field line, which brought the leadoff batter in. The score was now 1-0 in favor of Ithaca College.

Lake Forest was up to bat in the bottom of the sixth, and things got interesting.

With a runner on second base, Coach Pallozzi decided to switch pitchers. When the freshman pitcher came in, she walked the first batter but was able to get the next two batters out. She then gave up a single to left field.

As the inning evolved, the game quickly became 2-1, in favor of Lake Forest, due to an error. The key mistake had been made by the player who took Sarah's position. Sarah, who had fully assumed her new role, was watching for mistakes. She would tell her teammates ways for them to capitalize on any weakness that Lake Forest had.

While the team was down about the runs and when all hope seemed lost, Sarah emerged from the dugout screaming, "Coach, call time! Coach, call time-out!"

Coach Pallozzi took one look at her senior and did not hesitate to call time.

Before heading out toward the field, she asked Sarah why she was calling time. Sarah said that the batter had missed first base when she rounded and was on her way to second base. Coach Pallozzi walked out, appealed the play, and the first base umpire ruled the batter out. Because the runner missed the bag before the lead runner touched home plate, the second run did not count and neither did the first. Ithaca College was still up 1-0.

The game would go into the seventh inning and have a few more exciting moments, but it ended 1-0.

Ithaca College won its first—and to date only—national championship, all because of Sarah.

* * *

As much as I am sure Sarah was disappointed about losing her starting position, she made the most out of her situation and transitioned smoothly into her new role.

That's part of being on a team: adjusting when you have to.

Sarah could have been in the dugout cursing the player who stole her position.

She could have been pouting about being on the bench during the final game of her career.

She could have quit long before that moment ever happened.

Instead, she is the player who Coach Pallozzi credits with winning a national title.

Sarah knew and understood her new role and purpose for her team.

During Michelle Morgan's senior hockey season at St. Thomas, she knew her role and purpose. She did not have a great relationship with her coach, but she quickly realized she was not there for her coach. For Michelle, playing was all about being there for her teammates. She discovered her purpose in that sense.

"Sometimes you hear things that you do not want to hear, such as 'you're not playing' when you think you should be. I think this helps you realize that you're not always the smartest person in the room. You're not always the most talented person in the room. But you have to walk into that room knowing you can add value in certain ways and recognize that as a talent and a gift," Michelle stated.

Michelle has taken this idea of knowing your role and understanding your purpose into her professional career as well. She never thought she would end up back in college athletics, but an opportunity opened up at her alma mater and she took it. Michelle is now forever grateful for the opportunity she had because she feels as though she had found her calling. She feels fulfilled and like she has found her purpose.

If Michelle were never a student-athlete, she may not have understood the importance of knowing her role and purpose.

* * *

The concept of team is even incorporated into the Pyramid of Success—team spirit, specifically.

According to the Pyramid, "A genuine consideration for others. An eagerness to sacrifice personal interests of glory for the welfare of all."[58] When you assume your role on a team, this is essentially what you do. Wooden elaborated, "For me, it meant I was constantly searching for that player who would

---

58 Coach John Wooden. (2019). *Pyramid of Success - Coach John Wooden.*

make our team 'great' rather than a someone who was just a 'great player.'"[59]

Employers look for this quality as well. They want someone who is team-oriented and able to motivate those around them, not someone only looking out for their own interests.

Perhaps Cheryl Strayed said it best, in a quote Michelle echoed: "You don't have a right to the cards you believe you should have been dealt. You have an obligation to play the hell out of the ones you're holding."[60]

Uncover your role, find your purpose, and use it to drive yourself to be the best that you can be.

---

59 Ibid.
60 Women For One. (2017). *You don't have a right to the cards you believe you should have been dealt. You have an obligation to play the hell out of the ones you're holding. - Cheryl Strayed | Women For One.*

CHAPTER 13

BUILDING RELATIONSHIPS

———

Ask not what your teammates can do for you. Ask what you can do for your teammates.

—MAGIC JOHNSON, FIVE-TIME NBA CHAMPION[61]

One of the most challenging aspects of going to college is leaving behind your home, your family, and your friends. Essentially, everything you have known.

---

61   BrainyQuote. (n.d.). *Magic Johnson Quotes.*

I am not going to sugarcoat it: the transition from high school to college can be plagued with difficulty. It was for me, and I know it was for other student-athletes as well.

However, one of the benefits of being a student-athlete is that you have a team waiting for you as soon as you step on campus. I know that this fact was one selling point for me when it came to deciding to play softball in college.

Why wouldn't you want a group of people waiting to be friends with you?

I can remember the summer going into my freshman year, receiving an email from Lauren, one of my future teammates, who at that time was a rising junior on the team. You have no idea how excited I was to receive this email. Her message essentially welcomed me to the team and told me to reach out if I had any questions. I know I reached out to her with questions, and I am sure that every other incoming freshman on my team did too.

Opening and reading that email put me at ease during my hectic summer preparing for college.

Although Lauren's email did help to calm my nerves and get me excited, I would not say my freshman year was smooth sailing from that point on.

* * *

As a student-athlete in high school, most people know who you are. Again, you are a big fish in a small pond.

When you are a freshman in college, that dynamic changes. You become a small fish in a ginormous pond.

Envision the biggest pond you can think of. That is what college can feel like at first, and that's how it felt for me. I felt this way at a small school too.

You go from knowing everything and everyone to hardly knowing anything or anyone. That reality can be a tough pill to swallow.

You are going to feel lost at times during college, but that experience is completely normal. Everyone feels the same way, regardless of whether they admit it out loud.

Nothing is more intimidating than trying to put yourself out there and make new friends, but relationship-building is everything. You eventually become used to doing it and will have to continue doing it later in life too. Creating relationships with your teammates, classmates, professors, and peers can lead to teamwork in another form down the road. The connections and relationships you build as a student-athlete are valuable no matter where they come from, which is something Shamaree Brown can attest to.

Currently, Shamaree is the director of student-athlete programs & compliance at the Atlantic Coast Conference (ACC). He obtained this role through intriguing means.

Shamaree always possessed a strong passion for sports. He was a football student-athlete at Winston-Salem State University, a Division II institution in Winston-Salem, North Carolina. Because of his love for sports, he majored in sports management to help him land a career in an area he thoroughly enjoyed.

Initially, Shamaree had his sights set on being a sports agent. So, he did what any good student would do and obtained an internship with a local agent who worked primarily with football players. However, after his experience, Shamaree quickly discovered that the lifestyle of the job didn't fit his personality or his personal vision and goals for himself.

In an accidental and unfortunate way, Shamaree realized exactly what he wanted to do for the rest of his life.

Sadly for Shamaree, he suffered a knee injury at the beginning of his senior year, which ended up requiring surgery. Shamaree had to sit out the first four games of his final football season. Shamaree likes to keep busy, so he ended up volunteering to assist in operations at the football games on the weekends. Along with this new role, he was helping out in the athletic department during the week in any way he could.

Given his experience as a student-athlete and now an athletic administrator, Shamaree offers an interesting perspective on the student-athlete experience. When I asked him what tips he had for incoming freshman student-athletes, he instantly responded by noting the importance of relationship-building.

* * *

When you think of college athletics, I am almost positive that relationship-building isn't the first thing that comes to mind. Why would it?

However, as a college athlete, you are going to come in contact with many people between athletics, academics, and extracurriculars. Being a student-athlete is all about the relationships you build and how you utilize them.

Here's where the teamwork aspect of things comes into play.

Demonstrating teamwork in the classroom and on the field will naturally help relationships flourish.

Once you have established and built trust off of teamwork, your teammates become a part of your personal network. On the other side of this dynamic, you also become a part of their network.

Now, I am not saying that any person you interact with on your team or in class will automatically be on your side because that is certainly not realistic. But I am saying that the people you make connections with and keep in touch with from time to time are likely going to do whatever they can to help you. And you should do the same for them as well.

That's what networking is all about.

This relates to the Benjamin Franklin Effect. I first learned about this idea while I was reading Dr. Meg Jay's book *The Defining Decade*. Benjamin Franklin once said, "He that hath once done you a kindness will be more ready to do you another than he whom you yourself have obliged."

So, what does this statement mean?

We do not need to know someone very well for them to be a part of our network or do a favor for us. Dr. Jay explained, "If weak ties do favors for us, they start to like us. Then they become even more likely to grant us additional favors in the future. Franklin decided that if he wanted to get someone on his side, he ought to ask for a favor. And he did."[62]

Believe it or not, people love doing favors for one another. You see this time and time again in the professional workforce. "There is a 'helper's high' that comes from being generous. ... Most people remember starting out themselves, being helped by those who were further along. Because of this, there is a reserve of goodwill," Dr. Jay elaborated.

Sports are used as a vehicle to unite people. Odds are, you probably even have a connection with someone on an opposing team too. Use any connection you have to help leverage yourself and do the same when you have the chance to for someone else.

Shamaree Brown has a holistic perspective on the student-athlete experience.

When I asked him his overall goal for student-athletes in the ACC, first and foremost he said to graduate. Ultimately, finishing college should be the goal for all student-athletes.

Part two of his answer was to build relationships. "I think the value of the college experience is the relationships that you

---

62 Jay, M. (n.d.). The Defining Decade: Why Your Twenties Matter and How to Make the Most of Them Now.

build," Shamaree noted. He added that this means relationships with professors, administrators, staff members around campus, and most importantly students on campus, not just other athletes.

* * *

Reflecting on my freshman year of college, I had a challenging time because I did not focus on building relationships.

When I stepped onto campus, I was so excited to meet all my teammates—so excited that I only focused on becoming good friends with them, and only them. I was not interested in meeting other students because I thought my team was all that I would need.

Boy, was I wrong.

Although my team provided me with great friendships that I am forever thankful for, I was lacking outside interaction during my freshman year. If I had a bad day at softball, I had no way to escape it. I could always count on my teammates to pick me up, but something was missing.

When I came back from summer break ready to tackle sophomore year, I was determined to meet more people outside of athletics, and I did exactly that. I had to force myself to step outside of my comfort zone. For me, this meant joining a bunch of clubs and trying to be more active across campus.

I also started taking some classes outside of my major, which also introduced me to other students on campus I may otherwise have never met. Becoming more involved and meeting new people made me an overall happier person. Let me tell you, it is nice to be able to walk around campus and have people say hello to you by name. It made me feel good.

If I had continued down the path I was on my freshman year, I would have never experienced this phenomenon to the extent that I did.

* * *

As my conversation with Shamaree continued, he kept emphasizing how crucial relationship-building is, especially during your freshman year of college.

You should want everyone to know who you are, not only because you're a student-athlete, but because you take the time to meet and get to know people.

Having these relationships campuswide helps make your school feel like home, Shamaree added. "It makes your stay and your experience very impactful. You'll have lots of people who will be watching out for you," he said.

I can attest that there is no better feeling than this.

Additionally, you never know when you may need to draw on a connection with someone. Having preestablished relationships and continuing to keep in touch will assist you.

"When you build relationships, you also build into favors. People want to help you," Shamaree added.

The same should go for you.

You should want to help others you have built relationships with.

This advice goes back to building up your personal network. Shamaree advised that down the road, in five, ten, fifteen, or twenty years from now, you may have a classmate who is a successful business owner and you are connected to them now because you took the time to build the relationship.

This is networking in its simplest form.

* * *

When you are thrown into new surroundings, relationship-building can be challenging.

As I mentioned, most freshman student-athletes are coming from being a big fish in a small pond and transitioning into being the smallest of fish in the largest of ponds.

USA Today published a list of tips for building relationships in college. First of all, be yourself. Your relationships will not be genuine if you are putting on an act. Never lie to yourself just to agree with someone in an attempt to make a friend. The friendship won't end up working out, I can promise you that. Second, participate in extracurriculars. College campuses are full of opportunities such as clubs, intramurals, and more. Find something that suits you well.[63]

As a student-athlete, your schedule is already jampacked to begin with, but carving out a little extra time for extracurriculars is definitely worth it. Inviting someone to a meal is also an easy way to build a relationship. Some of my best friends in college were made by asking them if they wanted to grab dinner.

Believe it or not, friendship is even a part of the Pyramid of Success. It states, "Friendship comes from mutual esteem,

---

63   Goldman, J. (2012). *10 ways to make friends in college*. Usatoday.com.

respect, and devotion. Like marriage, it must not be taken for granted but requires a joint effort."[64] Your teammates are going to become your friends; it's inevitable. You spend so much time together, so it is natural that friendships will flourish. Some will even become more like family.

The key here is to keep up with those relationships.

When the season is over or after you graduate, continue to work on those relationships.

Do not take them for granted.

Now, Dr. Meg Jay told us that we do not necessarily need to know someone very well for them to help us and vice versa. But we do want to keep people like this in our network.

As a student-athlete, you are accustomed to meeting new people and quickly bonding to become a team.

In college and the professional workforce, take those skills to the next level and find the people who are going to enhance your network.

---

64 Coach John Wooden. (2019). *Pyramid of Success - Coach John Wooden.*

TEAMWORK TAKEAWAYS:

- Know your role and execute it to the best of your ability.
- Each member of the team serves a specific purpose.
- Build relationships.

PART III

UTILIZATION

CHAPTER 14

OWNING IT AS A FORMER ATHLETE

——

Today I will do what others won't, so tomorrow I can accomplish what others can't.

—JERRY RICE, THREE-TIME SUPER BOWL CHAMPION[65]

Unfortunately for all of us, the time will come when our student-athlete journey ends—a sad, harsh reality filled with many different emotions.

You know what they say: "You don't know what you've got until it's gone."

---

65 Goodreads.com. (n.d.). *A quote by Jerry Rice.*

The sport that has given you so much will no longer be playing as big a role in your life as it has for a number of years.

For some athletes, this transition is difficult initially. For most athletes, probably.

However, this is an obstacle you can certainly overcome.

* * *

Someone reach out to me via LinkedIn who was curious what exactly my book was about. We got to talking and he started telling me about his podcast for former collegiate student-athletes.

Matt Mounier is the founder of *The Untold 98 Percent*, a podcast that shares the stories of student-athletes and their transition into the real world after graduation. The podcast covers the major challenges and obstacles student-athletes face when searching for a career and starting their first job.

Matt was a Division III basketball player at Whitman College. When it came time for him to hang up his basketball shoes, he was confused as to what exactly his next step would be. Matt had a difficult time deciding between starting a career or going to play professional basketball overseas. Ultimately, he chose to pursue a career other than basketball, and he was searching left and right for that perfect opportunity.

During his quest, Matt noticed how his student-athlete experience listed on his resume helped him obtain interviews.

The problem, however, was that despite getting interviews, he couldn't lock down a job.

Matt became frustrated.

He thought getting a job as a former collegiate athlete would be easy, or at least he had always heard that. Matt thus had a bumpy transition from college to the real world, which is actually somewhat common.

Retiring from playing the sport you love isn't easy; it triggers a lot of emotions. When things aren't exactly going your way on the job front, you may stop and question everything. Fortunately, you were a student-athlete. You are used to facing adversity. You have accomplished so much during your time as a collegiate athlete, and you're more than ready to take on more.

Luckily for Matt, he landed a job that corresponded with his major, economics. Then, after excelling in that role, he transitioned into fully focusing on *The Untold 98 Percent*, which allowed him to develop the Transitioning Athlete Playbook, a one on one coaching platform to help create a smoother transition for athletes.

You have all the tools—you just need to figure out how best to utilize them.

* * *

That said, you will find numerous opportunities waiting for you as a former collegiate athlete; you just have to search for the right one. I'm not saying it will come easy. Matt's story is truly a testament that it doesn't. Searching for the right job opportunity is something you will have to work at. That one job posting that is right for someone else may not be right for you and vice versa, which is why it takes time to find the perfect job opportunity. A lot of it has to do with timing too. Timing is everything.

Believe it or not, as a student-athlete, you are sought after.

People are looking to bring you into their organization because they know what student-athletes are all about. You heard it straight from Beth Brooke-Marciniak, who said she would hire former student-athletes all day if she could.

Employers want you because they know athletes know how to **OWN IT**.

The concept I believe sums it up the best is "the student-athlete edge," which I learned from Antonio Neves.

As success goes, Antonio is truly self-made, something he attributes to being a collegiate athlete.

* * *

Now a speaker, author, and broadcast journalist, Antonio found that being a student-athlete was "a game-changer" for him.

He attended Western Michigan University and was able to walk onto their Division I track and field team. He knew he was not going to be a national champion or make it to the Olympics, but being a student-athlete was definitely something special to him because Antonio was a first-generation college student. Initially, he did not realize the numerous opportunities that college would provide him outside of his sport. Being a student-athlete allowed Antonio to learn about internship experiences, study abroad opportunities, and ways to get involved on campus while continuing to be a committed Division I athlete.

The busier the better is how Antonio sees it.

Being heavily involved on campus, along with being a Division I student-athlete, provided structure to his daily routine.

Although being an athlete naturally creates structure within a schedule, Antonio's additional activities took this organization to a whole new level. He would block off time every day for practices, workouts, classes, coursework, and extracurriculars. He never had to make any guesses; he always knew when he was going to accomplish what he needed to.

"A busy schedule actually created a really strong structure for me, and it created a strong discipline," Antonio told me.

Having a jampacked schedule also forced Antonio to constantly plan ahead, and naturally, planning ahead required good communication with his professors and coaches, which is a transferrable skill. Heather Ryan, executive director of academic services at Duke University, echoed this sentiment, pointing to how Antonio was able to take **OWN**ership of his education.

The opportunities that student-athletes receive can separate them from those of non-athletes—what Antonio refers to as "the student-athlete edge."

"Student-athletes walk away with the skillset that the standard college student does not walk away with," he pointed out. Antonio believes this happens because athletes know what it is like to be disciplined and structured. They also know how to be held accountable for their actions. Because of this "edge," Antonio feels as though athletes are more successful in their careers than non-athletes. He relates this effect back to the competitiveness that accompanies being an athlete.

"When student-athletes step into companies, they're already prepared to win. They are prepared to succeed in a way that students who were not athletes struggle with early on in their career. But athletes are ready to hit the ground running," Antonio explained.

This philosophy ties back to Antonio's thoughts on the importance of being busy. Having a busy schedule as a student-athlete not only teaches discipline but also prepares you for the professional workforce.

* * *

Studies have analyzed the value college athletics possesses and how it can help to prepare student-athletes for their future careers.

One study found that the most common skills gained through athletic participation include discipline, dedication, sacrifice, integrity, leadership, teamwork, work ethic, and drive to succeed.[66] When it comes to hiring decisions, employers seek

---

66   Foy Moore, E. (2017). *A COMPARISON OF WORK ETHIC AMONG HIGH SCHOOL ATHLETES AND NON-ATHLETES.* Pdfs.semanticscholar.org.

candidates who have strong interpersonal skills along with extracurriculars.[67] College athletics provides athletes with both of these.

The professional workforce is a lot like a sports team, actually. Each person has a specific role that contributes to the overall goals of the company. In addition, companies are broken up into several different teams that each have their own goals for helping the company. A lot of companies are very team-oriented, an environment in which student-athletes tend to naturally thrive given their experience.

Playing sports, in general, will teach you a lot of things about yourself. You will also learn a lot about life in general. Playing a sport in college takes this education to the next level.

Significant research conducted on this topic has weighed the benefits that college athletics can provide. According to the National Scouting Report, playing sports collegiately helps prepare you for the real world. This includes intangible skills, lessons learned, and relationships.[68] All these benefits are captured within **OWN IT**. Intangible skills include discipline, confidence, leadership, and time management. Obviously,

---

67   Barison, J. (2017). *What Are the Top Skills Employers Look for in a Candidate? - Careers in Government*. Careers in Government.

68   Rondeau, S. (2016). *3 Benefits of Playing College Sports | National Scouting Report*. National Scouting Report.

these skills can be acquired over time, but student-athletes come into their professional careers with these already in their tool belt.

The lessons that sports teach help former student-athletes understand how to deal with adversity in various aspects of their lives. At the same time, the relationships you build through sports will be lifelong ones. And, through building these relationships, you gain the skill of maintaining relationships with others. Relationship-building is an important skill in the professional workforce too.

The **OWN IT** structure is more than applicable to your life post-athletics. Using the skills and characteristics you developed as a college athlete will help you to navigate your life after college.

Doing so is what makes former student-athletes so successful.

I am not saying that it is going to be smooth sailing from here, but you are more than prepared and equipped to take on your next journey.

CHAPTER 15

TIME TO OWN IT

The more difficult the victory, the greater the happiness in winning.

—WAYNE GRETZKY, LEADING SCORER IN NHL HISTORY[69]

Now you are officially ready to **OWN IT**.

You're ready to **OWN IT** in several areas:

- The classroom,
- The field/court,
- The professional workforce.

---

[69] Bright Drops. (n.d.). 55 Most Famous Inspirational Sports Quotes of All-Time.

Use the experiences from me and others, along with the research provided, to help you navigate your precious time as a student-athlete and your life afterward.

You'll be surprised how athletics can prepare you for various opportunities outside of your sport.

So let's recap:

We **OWN IT** by understanding and implementing

- **O**penness
- **W**illpower
- **N**erve
- **I**ntrospection
- **T**eamwork

* * *

O

Through **OPENNESS,** we practice stepping outside our comfort zone to help us grow. Think about Ryan Gilliam, the former USF football player who was able to find success elsewhere after his NFL dreams were crushed. Ryan would have never been able to accomplish all that he has without being open to different opportunities outside of football.

Having the openness to step outside of your comfort zone will teach you many things about yourself. Not only will you discover your strengths and weaknesses, you will also uncover your passions. That's how it worked for Lee Reed. He remained open to new professional opportunities until he found the one he felt most passionate about and fulfilled by. Become comfortable with being uncomfortable.

W

Use **WILLPOWER** to take control of your actions. As a student-athlete, be prepared to face adversity and use your willpower to overcome whatever obstacle is in your way. Dominique Moceanu was faced with one hurdle after another and refused to give up or back down. Her demonstration of willpower in several instances is truly inspiring. Being challenged is not a bad thing. Use challenges to help you shape your character; each one is a new learning experience.

Willpower also encompasses the ability to make sacrifices. As athletes, we have been doing this since day one. Unfortunately, we can't do it all, although most of us wish we could. For student-athletes, it always feels as though there aren't enough hours in a day. That's why we have to make sacrifices and doing so takes willpower. Keep the college student triangle image ingrained in your mind and think about how you have to juggle athletics on top of everything else. It's not easy, so use your willpower to help guide you.

N

Find your **NERVE**. Nerve and willpower go hand in hand. Willpower helps you demonstrate nerve. The easiest way for you to find your nerve is by setting goals for yourself. Don't forget to **OWN** your education as well, just as Heather Ryan encouraged us to do. Take ownership by setting goals for yourself and use your nerve to accomplish them.

Speaking up for what you believe in also ties into this aspect. You must have courage in the form of confidence. Think about the confidence that Beth Brooke-Marciniak needed in herself to be part of the first female class to be on athletic scholarship. Sports help teach and build confidence, an important trait for life post athletics. Like I said, demonstrate nerve, be confident in yourself, and have the courage to do what others can't.

I

INTROSPECTION is something you may not find necessary, but it definitely makes a difference. Try it and you'll see. Reflect on yourself to uncover what you did not initially realize or understand. Doing so will allow you to make self-improvements in more ways than one. Introspection applies to every aspect of your life, but it can really enhance your experience as a student-athlete.

One of the most valuable lessons introspection can teach is that being a student-athlete is a privilege. Once you understand this idea, you'll be doing everything you can to make the most of your experience. For Jenna Lilley, this meant combining her academic and athletic passions, a feat made possible by her understanding the connection between the two through introspection.

T

As cliché as it is, **TEAMWORK** truly does make the dream work. On every team, each person has a designated and specific role. Knowing and understanding your role is critical. Each person on a team serves a specific purpose. Make it your goal to understand your purpose and do what you can to help the team succeed. Your team values you, so don't forget to value yourself.

I truly believe Cheryl Strayed said it perfectly: "You don't have a right to the cards you believe you should have been dealt. You have an obligation to play the hell out of the ones you're holding." Along with this notion, find the value in each and every one of your teammates. Continue to work to build strong, long-lasting relationships with every member of your team. This method is networking in the purest sense, and it will help you in the professional work world as well.

The time has come for you to go out and **OWN IT** in everything you do. Use each letter of **OWN IT** to make the most of each and every experience you take on.

The student-athlete experience is one like no other.

Make the most of it and use it to help you successfully navigate your career and life.

CONCLUSION

You have heard from many individuals who were in your shoes at one point in time. Hindsight is 20/20, and now they realize the positive impact that being a student-athlete can have.

In the moment, you may not feel as though you are benefitting from your time as a student-athlete. In fact, you may even feel as though you are wasting your time if things aren't going your way. No one said being a student-athlete was easy.

Feeling this way is okay. It happens to everyone at some point in time.

Let's face it: if it were easy, everyone would do it. But you will look back on the hardest times and maybe even end up enjoying them the most.

Just know that your time as a student-athlete will affect you for the rest of your life—and in a positive way, might I add. The student-athlete experience is truly something special and unique. You are a part of a very select group of people who get the chance to have this opportunity. This fact separates you from the general population.

Now, by no means am I saying you are superior to others.

What I am saying, though, is that you now have a unique experience paired with a skill set that makes you different. Use these tools to leverage yourself.

Regardless of what sport you play or what division your school is in, you worked hard to get to where you are.

You're not done yet. You have so many new opportunities waiting for you, some of which you most likely do not even realize exist yet.

Use your experience as a student-athlete to drive you to discover success elsewhere.

The cool thing about the **OWN IT** structure is that it applies to a variety of people. Whether you are:

- A future college athlete,
- A current student-athlete,
- A former student-athlete,

You can **OWN IT**.

This structure applies to you and is designed to help you succeed in your career and life.

So you've finished this book.

Now what?

Future college athletes, don't blink. Four years of eligibility go quick and you can't get them back. From reading this book, you have an idea of what to expect of your collegiate student-athlete experience. You now know some tactical ways to make the most out of your time as a student-athlete. You have heard from people who have been there. Use their experiences as a guide to prepare for your time as a college athlete.

Current student-athletes, congratulations. You made it! Do not take this opportunity for granted and do what you can to make it count. You know it's not an easy journey, so take each challenge you face during your time as an athlete as a learning experience. Each obstacle you overcome prepares you for your life post-athletics. Find balance in being a student and an athlete so that you can make the most out of the time left in your journey.

Former student-athletes, we are all in the same boat. Of course, we miss playing our sport. It was such a large part of our lives for so long. However, we can find opportunities out there waiting for us. Seek out your right opportunity and **OWN IT**. Use your experiences from your time as a student-athlete to motivate and leverage yourself in other areas of your life. You have all the tools; you just have to use them right.

Athletic administrators, be there for your athletes. You have the chance to make an impact in the lives of each student-athlete who steps foot on your campus. You know and understand that the chances of them becoming professional athletes are slim to none. Enhance their time as a student-athlete so that they can use their experiences to help them later in life in whatever career path they choose.

Parents of student-athletes, your constant support will always be appreciated. You have been there since day one and your student-athlete will need you to be there up until the final buzzer or the last out. The transitions from high school to college and then college to the real world are challenging. No one understands like you the potential that your student-athlete has. Help them find success in the classroom, on the court, and in the professional world.

So, what are you waiting for?

You can't **OWN IT** by just sitting here.

Get up and implement the **OWN IT** structure into your daily life. Through your student-athlete experience, you have been given the tools to succeed. Now all you need to do is use your experience to help you find the success that you're looking for.

Regardless of whatever stage of your life you are in, you are ready to take the reins on your experiences and use them to your advantage.

Now that you understand how to **OWN IT**, here's my challenge to you:

Think about each component of the **OWN IT** structure and set realistic goals for yourself that are going to help you **OWN IT** now, as well as in the future.

You've **OWN**ed this book. Now it's time for you to get out there and **OWN IT**.

ACKNOWLEDGMENTS

—

Never in a million years did I ever think that I would write a book. But the best things come when we least expect them, and I am so glad that I was presented with this unique opportunity. When setting out on this long journey, I had no idea how much work it would take to get to publication, but what I discovered is that publishing a book truly takes a village, and I am so grateful for all of the support.

First and foremost, I want to thank my family. Mom, Dad, and Carolyn, your constant support in each and every one of my endeavors does not go unnoticed. Whether it was school, softball, this book, or any other of my crazy ideas, you were always there pushing me to be my best.

Thank you to Eric Koester and his program, Creator Institute, for giving me this opportunity to write and publish this book. What you are doing for college students across the country is truly inspiring. Special thanks to Doan Winkel and the John Carroll University Entrepreneurship Department. Doan, you taught me so much about entrepreneurship, professionalism, and myself. Our forty-five-minute workshops every Monday were some of the most valuable moments of my college career.

I also want to thank Brian Bies and my editors, Jordan Water-wash, Stephanie McKibben, and everyone else at New Degree Press who helped bring this book to life. Your support and guidance along the way was critical to the publication of this book.

A big thank you to everyone who gave me their time for a personal interview. The stories you shared and the advice you gave is going to help future, current, and former student-athletes everywhere.

Finally, thank you to each person who contributed to my pre-order campaign. You have no idea how much your support along this journey means to me.

Amy Berresford*	Athena Kalogeris
Amy & Andy Lucas	Becky & Tom Wild*
Angie Zappitelli	Bev & Bob Barron

Brooke Beck

Calvin Long

Cam Gerard

Carolyn Cook*

Cassandra Jameyson

Charles Zammerilla*

Christopher Papalia

Claire Kelly

Cooper Lando

Diane DePasquale

Doan Winkel*

Eric Koester

Grant Wilson

Giulia & Jim O'Keeffe

Hannah Floss

Jacob Schupp

Jeana Franjoine

Jen Turko

Jenn Patterson

Jill & Jim Krally

John Tucci

Joseph Papalia

Judy Rosenhoover

Julia Sherwin

Katie O'Connell

Kim & Ben Read

Lauren & Chart Westcott*

Liz O'Grady

Logan Vignovic

Lou Ann & Bob Cook*

Maggie LaForce

Mark Grabowski

Mark Weaver*

Matthew Kotkiewicz*

Michele & Bill Zammerilla*

Michele & Jack Klingler

Nicholas Wilson

Pam Wrobleski*

Ron Kotkiewicz*

Ruth & John Belhumeur

Shari & Lou Vojtash

Sherry & Courtney Cox

Sophie Yankto

Taylor Evans

Key:
* indicates multiple copies purchased

APPENDIX

———

INTRODUCTION

1. NCAA.org - The Official Site of the NCAA. (n.d.). *Student-Athletes.* [online] Available at: http://www.ncaa.org/student-athletes [Accessed 22 Sep. 2019].

2. Parker, T. (2019). *What Does the NCAA Really Net from March Madness?*.[online] Investopedia. Available at: https://www.investopedia.com/articles/investing/031516/how-much-does-ncaa-make-march-madness.asp [Accessed 22 Sep. 2019].

3. NCAA.org - The Official Site of the NCAA. (n.d.). *Student-Athletes.* [online] Available at: http://www.ncaa.org/student-athletes [Accessed 22 Sep. 2019].

4. NCAA.org. (2018). [online] Available at: https://www.ncaa.org/sites/default/files/Recruiting%20Fact%20Sheet%20WEB.pdf [Accessed 22 Sep. 2019].

5. Gilliam, R. (2018). *Tallahassee Dreams.* [video] Available at: https://www.youtube.com/watch?v=p9eXsuOrdeY. [Accessed 22 Sep. 2019].

6. NCAA TV Commercial, 'Opportunity' Featuring Jerry Rice. (2016). [image] Available at: https://www.ispot.tv/ad/AMap/ncaa-opportunity-featuring-jerry-rice [Accessed 22 Sep. 2019].

7. Gilliam, R. (2018). *Tallahassee Dreams.* [video] Available at: https://www.youtube.com/watch?v=p9eXsuOrdeY. [Accessed 22 Sep. 2019].

8. Johnson, H. (2018). *A look at the link between playing sports and success in business.* [online] The CEO Magazine. Available at: https://www.theceomagazine.com/business/management-leadership/look-link-playing-sports-success-business/ [Accessed 22 Sep. 2019].

CHAPTER 1: DUMB JOCK

9. Competitive Advantage: Mental Toughness. (n.d.). Competitive Advantage Sports Quote. [online] Available at: https://www.competitivedge.com/quote-2166 [Accessed 22 Sep. 2019].

10. Barrett, J. (2017). The Equinox – The stereotype of athletes: Dumb Jock Syndrome. [online]

11. Feltz, D., Schneider, R., Hwang, S. and Skogsberg, N. (2013). Predictors of Collegiate Student-Athletes'' Susceptibility to Stereotype Threat. Journal of College Student Development, 54(2), pp.184-201.

12. Buhler, D. (n.d.). The Most Common Stereotypes About Student Athletes, Debunked. [online] Study Breaks. Available at: https://studybreaks.com/college/student-athletes/ [Accessed 22 Sep. 2019].

13. Sheingold, D. (2017). NCAA basketball: Graduation rates for all 64 tournament teams. [online] Northjersey.com. Available at: https://www.northjersey.com/story/sports/college/basketball/2017/03/23/ncaa-march-madness-graduation-rates/99548086/ [Accessed 22 Sep. 2019].

14. Anon, (2015). [image] Available at: https://imgur.com/gallery/IarOHAH [Accessed 22 Sep. 2019].

15. Ncaa.org. (2018). [online] Available at: https://www.ncaa.org/sites/default/files/Recruiting%20Fact%20Sheet%20WEB.pdf [Accessed 22 Sep. 2019].

16. Kniffin, K., Wansink, B. and Shimizu, M. (2014). Sports at Work. Journal of Leadership & Organizational Studies, 22(2), pp.217-230.

17. USA TODAY High School Sports. (2017). 6 reasons former athletes find success after college. [online] Available at: https://usatodayhss.com/2017/6-reasons-former-athletes-find-success-after-college [Accessed 22 Sep. 2019].

18. Krings, M. (2014). Study shows high school athletes perform better in school, persist to graduation more than non-athletes. [online] The University of Kansas. Available at: https://news.ku.edu/2014/01/15/study-shows-high-school-athletes-performed-better-school-persisted-graduation-more-non [Accessed 22 Sep. 2019].

19. ScholarshipStats.com. (n.d.). Odds of playing a college sport from high school. [online] Available at: http://www.scholarshipstats.com/varsityodds.html [Accessed 22 Sep. 2019].

CHAPTER 2: OWNING THE STUDENT-ATHLETE EXPERIENCE

20. Stricherz, A. (n.d.). Words John Wooden Never Used. [Blog] Sports & Spirituality. Available at: http://sportsandspirituality.blogspot.com/2015/08/words-john-wooden-never-used.html [Accessed 22 Sep. 2019].

21. John Wooden: The difference between winning and succeeding. (2001). [video] Available at: https://www.ted.com/talks/john_wooden_on_the_difference_between_winning_and_success?language=en [Accessed 22 Sep. 2019].

22. Ibid.

23. Ncaa.org. (n.d.). Countable Athletically Relatable Activities. [online] Available at: https://www.ncaa.org/sites/default/files/20-Hour-Rule-Document.pdf [Accessed 22 Sep. 2019].

24. USA TODAY High School Sports. (2017). 6 reasons former athletes find success after college. [online] Available at: https://usatodayhss.com/2017/6-reasons-former-athletes-find-success-after-college [Accessed 22 Sep. 2019].

25. www.dictionary.com. (n.d.). Definition of willpower | Dictionary.com. [online] Available at: https://www.dictionary.com/browse/willpower [Accessed 22 Sep. 2019].

CHAPTER 3: OPENNESS

26. What's Possible... (n.d.). *Favorite Quotes*. [online] Available at: https://afuntanilla.wordpress.com/favorite-quotes/ [Accessed 22 Sep. 2019].

27. Gilliam, R. (2018). Tallahassee Dreams. [video] Available at: https://www.youtube.com/watch?v=p9eXsuOrdeY. [Accessed 22 Sep. 2019].

CHAPTER 4: OPEN FOR THE FUTURE

28. Wiepert, G. (2013). https://www.si.com. [online] SI.com. Available at: https://www.si.com/nfl/2013/01/15/tim-tebow-future-uncertain [Accessed 22 Sep. 2019]

29. Nces.ed.gov. (2017). Beginning College Students Who Change Their Majors Within 3 Years of Enrollment. [online] Available at: https://nces.ed.gov/pubs2018/2018434.pdf [Accessed 22 Sep. 2019].

30. Rosenberg McKay, D. (2019). How Often Do People Change Careers?. [online] The Balance Careers. Available at: https://www.thebalancecareers.com/how-often-do-people-change-careers-3969407 [Accessed 22 Sep. 2019].

31. Coach John Wooden. (2019). *Pyramid of Success - Coach John Wooden*. [online] Available at: https://www.thewoodeneffect.com/pyramid-of-success/ [Accessed 3 Oct. 2019].

32. Cawsey, B. (2016). How to apply Coach John Wooden''s Pyramid of Success principles to running. [Blog] Bri Cawsey. Available at: https://bricawsey.com/2016/10/apply-coach-john-woodens-pyramid-success-principles-running/ [Accessed 22 Sep. 2019

CHAPTER 5: WILLPOWER

33. BrainyQuote. (n.d.). Arnold Palmer Quotes. [online] Available at: https://www.brainyquote.com/quotes/arnold_palmer_134114 [Accessed 22 Sep. 2019].

34. Hobson, W. (2018). Larry Nassar, former USA Gymnastics doctor, sentenced to 40-175 years for sex crimes. The Washington Post. [online] Available at: https://www.washingtonpost.com/sports/olympics/larry-nassar-former-usa-gymnastics-doctor-due-to-be-sentenced-for-sex-crimes/2018/01/24/9acc22f8-0115-11e8-8acf ad2991367d9d_story.html [Accessed 22 Sep. 2019].

35. WTOP. (2019). *Davis sets record at 0 for 49, including warning track shot | WTOP*. [online] Available at: https://wtop.com/baltimore-orioles/2019/04/davis-sets-record-by-going-hitless-in-47-straight-at-bats/ [Accessed 4 Oct. 2019].

36. Smith, C. (n.d.). 5 Things About Overcoming Adversity That Athletes Can Teach Entrepreneurs. [online] Athlete Network. Available at: https://an.athletenetwork.com/blog/5-things-about-overcoming-adversity-that-athletes-can-teach-entrepreneurs [Accessed 22 Sep. 2019].

CHAPTER 6: WILLING TO SACRIFICE

37. BrainyQuote. (n.d.). Kareem Abdul-Jabbar Quotes. [online] Available at: https://www.brainyquote.com/quotes/kareem_abduljabbar_370653 [Accessed 22 Sep. 2019].

38. Arvin, M. (2012). College Triangle. [online] WordPress. Available at: https://matthewarvin.wordpress.com/2012/12/03/study-finds-that-a-lack-of-sleep-results-in-weight-gain/college-triangle/ [Accessed 22 Sep. 2019].

39. Coach John Wooden. (2019). *Pyramid of Success - Coach John Wooden.* [online] Available at: https://www.thewoodeneffect.com/pyramid-of-success/ [Accessed 3 Oct. 2019].

CHAPTER 7: NERVE

40. BrainyQuote. (n.d.). John Wooden Quotes. [online] Available at: https://www.brainyquote.com/quotes/john_wooden_384233 [Accessed 22 Sep. 2019].

41. www.dictionary.com. (n.d.). Definition of nerving | Dictionary.com. [online] Available at: https://www.dictionary.com/browse/nerving [Accessed 22 Sep. 2019].

42. Pennington, B. (2008). It"s Not an Adventure, It"s a Job. [online] Nytimes.com. Available at: https://www.nytimes.com/2008/03/12/sports/12lifestyles.html [Accessed 22 Sep. 2019].

CHAPTER 8: NERVE TO COURAGE TO CONFIDENCE

43. Goodreads.com. (n.d.). A Quote by Michael Jordan. [online] Available at: https://www.goodreads.com/quotes/137783-you-must-expect-great-things-of-yourself-before-you-can [Accessed 22 Sep. 2019].

44. Lexico Dictionaries | English. (n.d.). Courage | Definition of Courage by Lexico. [online] Available at: https://www.oxforddictionaries.com/definition/english/courage [Accessed 22 Sep. 2019].

45. www2.ed.gov. (2015). Title IX and Sex Discrimination. [online] Available at: https://www2.ed.gov/about/offices/list/ocr/docs/tix_dis.html [Accessed 22 Sep. 2019].

46. Blue, K. and Criag, R. (2019). College athletes beating the odds in career quest. [online] The Hechinger Report. Available at: https://hechingerreport.org/opinion-college-athletics-departments-do-better-job-counseling-students/ [Accessed 22 Sep. 2019].

47. Taylor, D. (2011). Confidence Matters for Athletes. [online] Huffpost.com. Available at: https://www.huffpost.com/entry/confidence-matters-for-at_b_827666 [Accessed 22 Sep. 2019].

48. Coach John Wooden. (2019). *Pyramid of Success - Coach John Wooden.* [online] Available at: https://www.thewoodeneffect.com/pyramid-of-success/ [Accessed 3 Oct. 2019].

49. Coachwooden.com. (2019). *Official Site of Coach Wooden.* [online] Available at: http://www.coachwooden.com/pyramid-of-success#Pyramid/1 [Accessed 4 Oct. 2019].

CHAPTER 9: INTROSPECTION

50. A-Z Quotes. (n.d.). Jonathan Horton Quote. [online] Available at: https://www.azquotes.com/quote/552905 [Accessed 22 Sep. 2019].

CHAPTER 10: REFLECTING ON THE PRIVILEGE

51. Goodreads.com. (n.d.). A quote by Andre Agassi. [online] Available at: https://www.goodreads.com/quotes/351922-what-makes-something-special-is-not-just-what-you-have [Accessed 22 Sep. 2019].

52. NCAA.org - The Official Site of the NCAA. (n.d.). Student-Athletes. [online] Available at: http://www.ncaa.org/student-athletes [Accessed 22 Sep. 2019].

53. Corona, Z. (2014). 36 Reasons Why 33% of College Athletes Quit, Get Cut or Get Asked To Leave!. [Blog] *BeRecruited.* Available at: https://new.berecruited.com/athletes/521209/blog/011314-36-reasons-why-33-of-college-athletes-quit-cut-or-get-asked-to-leave [Accessed 4 Oct. 2019].

CHAPTER 11: INTROSPECT TO CONNECT

54. Wild Child Sports. (n.d.). Sports Quotes - 10 Quotes Every Athlete Must Read - Wild Child Sports. [online] Available at: https://wildchildsports.com/sports-quotes-10-quotes-every-athlete-must-read/ [Accessed 22 Sep. 2019].

55. NCAA.org - The Official Site of the NCAA. (n.d.). NCAA Student-Athlete Advisory Committees (SAACs). [online] Available at: http://www.ncaa.org/student-athletes/ncaa-student-athlete-advisory-committees-saacs [Accessed 22 Sep. 2019].

CHAPTER 12: TEAMWORK

56. Freeland, G. (2018). Talent Wins Games, Teamwork Wins Championships. [online] Forbes.com. Available at: https://www.forbes.com/sites/grantfreeland/2018/06/01/talent-wins-games-teamwork-wins-championships/#27b5d81f4c8f [Accessed 22 Sep. 2019].

57. Leading Essentially. (2018). The Story of Bill and Swen. [online] Available at: https://leadingessentially.com/2013/04/14/heres-to-swen/ [Accessed 22 Sep. 2019].

58. Coach John Wooden. (2019). *Pyramid of Success - Coach John Wooden.* [online] Available at: https://www.thewoodeneffect.com/pyramid-of-success/ [Accessed 3 Oct. 2019].

59. IBid

60. Women For One. (2017). *You don't have a right to the cards you believe you should have been dealt. You have an obligation to play the hell out of the ones you're holding. - Cheryl Strayed | Women For One.* [online] Available at: https://womenforone.com/portfolio/dont-right-cards-believe-dealt-obligation-play-hell-ones-youre-holding-cheryl-strayed/ [Accessed 22 Sep. 2019].

CHAPTER 13: BUILDING RELATIONSHIPS

61. BrainyQuote. (n.d.). Magic Johnson Quotes. [online] Available at: https://www.brainyquote.com/quotes/magic_johnson_131375 [Accessed 23 Sep. 2019].

62. Jay, M. (n.d.). The Defining Decade: Why Your Twenties Matter and How to Make the Most of Them Now.

63. Goldman, J. (2012). 10 ways to make friends in college. [online] Usatoday.com. Available at: https://www.usatoday.com/story/college/2012/07/30/10-ways-to-make-friends-in-college/37396027/ [Accessed 23 Sep. 2019].

64. Coach John Wooden. (2019). *Pyramid of Success - Coach John Wooden.* [online] Available at: https://www.thewoodeneffect.com/pyramid-of-success/ [Accessed 3 Oct. 2019].

CHAPTER 14: OWNING IT AS A FORMER STUDENT-ATHLETE

65. Goodreads.com. (n.d.). A quote by Jerry Rice. [online] Available at: https://www.goodreads.com/quotes/197367-today-i-will-do-what-others-won-t-so-tomorrow-i [Accessed 23 Sep. 2019].

66. Foy Moore, E. (2017). A COMPARISON OF WORK ETHIC AMONG HIGH SCHOOL ATHLETES AND NON-ATHLETES. [online] Pdfs.semanticscholar.org. Available at: https://pdfs.semanticscholar.org/b275/994897e629c5dfdf-1b373e4738b3a512f062.pdf [Accessed 23 Sep. 2019].

67. Barison, J. (2017). What Are the Top Skills Employers Look for in a Candidate? - Careers in Government. [online] Careers in Government. Available at: https://careersingovernment.com/tools/gov-talk/career-advice/top-skills-employers-look-candidate/ [Accessed 23 Sep. 2019].

68. Rondeau, S. (2016). 3 Benefits of Playing College Sports | National Scouting Report. [online] National Scouting Report. Available at: https://www.nsr-inc.com/scouting-news/3-benefits-of-playing-college-sports/ [Accessed 23 Sep. 2019].

CHAPTER 15: TIME TO OWN IT

69. Bright Drops. (n.d.). 55 Most Famous Inspirational Sports Quotes of All-Time. [online] Available at: https://brightdrops.com/inspirational-sports-quotes [Accessed 23 Sep. 2019].

Made in the USA
Monee, IL
06 December 2019